Light Can Change Everything

I AM THE WAY THE TRUTH AND THE LIFE
JOHN 14:6

Jacquelene Lofton

God bless you!
&
Keep you in perfect
peace !

Light Can Change Everything

DAY SELAH DEVOTIONAL

By
Jacqueline Lofton
and
Elaine Swaby

E-BookTime, LLC
Montgomery, Alabama

Light Can Change Everything
Day Selah Devotional

Copyright © 2006 by Jacqueline Lofton and Elaine Swaby

ISBN: 1-59824-360-8

First Edition
Published October 2006
E-BookTime, LLC
6598 Pumpkin Road
Montgomery, AL 36108
www.e-booktime.com

JANUARY 1

God's Plan: The Beginning

John 1:1

In the beginning was the Word, and the Word was with God, and the Word was God.

Genesis 1:1-5 (NIV)

[1] In the beginning God created the heavens and the earth.
[2] Now the earth was a formless and empty, darkness was over the surface of the deep, and the Spirit of God was hovering over the waters.
[3] And God said, "Let there be light," and there was light. [4] God saw that the light was good, and He separated the light from the darkness. [5] God called the light "day," and the darkness he called "night." And there was evening, and there was morning—the first day.

(New Year's Day)

JANUARY 2

God's Plan

But the Comforter (Counselor, Helper, Intercessor, Advocate, Strengthener, Standby), the Holy Spirit, whom the father will send in my name (in <u>my</u> place, to represent <u>me</u> and act on my behalf), he will teach you all things. And he will cause you to recall (will remind you of, bring to your remembrance) everything I have told you.

John 14:26 (AMP)

JANUARY 3

God's Plan

Thank you God, the Creator of this beautiful place,
Which is comprised of many race,
In which you give us all your grace.

Thank you for the Trinity.
We have only one true God, the Father, the sole divinity.
One Lord and Savior Jesus Christ, your only begotten son.
The Holy Spirit, the comforter.

Oh thank you for Jesus who went to Calvary and
Died on the cross for a great cause.

They nailed his feet,
They nailed his hands,
They pierced his sides.

JANUARY 4

God's Plan

He shed his blood,
For our love,
As he hung from the cross way above.

Thank you for suffering and dying on the cross,
So that we would not be lost,
Oh my dear Savior, what a cost.

Oh Jesus, blessed Savior,
Thank you for your favor,
Having your sweetness is a desirable flavor.
And one thing for sure you are my Savior.
Thank you Jesus for never leaving us,
Nor deceiving us.
Or misleading us.

JANUARY 5

The Kingdom of God

Matthew 6:10 & Daniel 2:44

"Your kingdom come…In the time of those kings, the God of heaven will set up a kingdom that will never be destroyed, nor will it be left to another people, it will crush all those kingdoms and bring them to an end, but it will itself endure forever."
Amen

The Lord has spoken!!!!

JANUARY 6

The Gift

For God so loved the world, that he gave his only begotten Son, that whosoever believeth in him should not perish, but have everlasting life.

John 3:16-17

JANUARY 7

The Gift

<u>G</u>od is the gift of life.

<u>I</u>ntegrity is what a man needs.

<u>F</u>aith is what we walk by.

<u>T</u>rust is what we have in God.

Therefore God gave us a gift, his son Jesus.
In Jesus lies integrity which is the gift that man needs.
And faith is the gift to believe and walk by.

And trust is the gift to count on God and our Lord and
Savior Jesus Christ, who is the gift of life.

JANUARY 8

Stewards of What God Has (Given) Birth Us With

Like good stewards of the manifold grace of God, serve one another with whatever gift each of you has received.
1 Peter 4:10 (NRSV)

JANUARY 9

Stewards of What God Has (Given) Birth Us With

As every man hat received the gift, even so <u>minister</u> the
same one to another, as good <u>stewards</u> of the
manifold grace of God.
1 Peter 4:10

JANUARY 10

Stewards of What God Has (Given) Birth Us With

God has given each of you some special <u>abilities</u>; be sure to
use them to help each other, passing on to others, God's
many kinds of blessings.
1 Peter 4:10 (TLB)

JANUARY 11

Stewards of What God Has (Given) Birth Us With

Are you called to preach? Then preach as though God himself were speaking through you. Are you called to help each other? Do it with all strength and energy that God supplies, so that God will be glorified.
1 Peter 4:11 (TLB)

JANUARY 12

Stewards of What God Has (Given) Birth Us With

Through Jesus Christ to him be glory and power forever and
ever. Amen.
1 Peter 4:11

JANUARY 13

Stewards of What God Has (Given) Birth Us With

Mother Theresa said:

What you are doing I may not be able to do.

What I'm doing you may not be able to do.

But all of us together are doing something beautiful for God. Amen.

> The gift of God is eternal life.
> **Romans 6:23**

JANUARY 14

Stewards of What God Has (Given) Birth Us With

Gift – something given to show friendship, affection, support, etc. The act, power, or right of giving, a natural ability.

Talent – to present with or as a gift.

For God so loved the whole world that he gave his only
begotten Son (Jesus) as a gift to us!!!
John 3:16

JANUARY 15

Who Are The Ministry Gifts Given To?

Yet each and (everyone), every believer in the body of
Christ is given a gift.
Ephesians 4:7

Not to acknowledge a gift from God Almighty is not a sign
of humility but rather of in gratitude. For this reason we
need to be careful not to down play God's gifts of grace in
our lives.

Pastors are not the only one's who do the work of the
ministry.

Their job is to prepare God's people to minister.

The "real" ministers are the people in the pews.

(Martin Luther King Day)

JANUARY 16

Who Are The Ministry Gifts Given To?

Church leaders minister by training and preparing the other ministers to use their spiritual gifts to serve others (1 Peter 4:10) so that the body of Christ is built up and grows towards "the whole measure of the fullness of Christ" **(Ephesians 4:13).**

JANUARY 17

Who Are The Ministry Gifts Given To?

We have been gifted in ways that make use necessary to others. Others have been gifted in ways that make them necessary to us. Some of us have special gifts for teaching others about God. Others may have the gift for hurting people. Our individual gifts are important for the emotional and spiritual growth of others. God has a purpose for each us, so we must strive to know him better through prayer and meditation on his Word. He will show us what our gifts are and how we can use them to help others. As we share our gifts and receive the benefits of other people's gifts, we will find the body of Christ growing stronger and full of love.

Grace is undeserved favor.
Hebrews 4:16

The Gift of Grace

Grace is created by God and given to man. On the basis of this point alone, Christianity is set apart from any other religion in the world. Every other approach to God is a bartering system; if I do this, God will do that. I'm either saved by works (what I do), emotions (what I experience), or knowledge (what I know).

By contrast, Christianity has no whiff of negotiation at all. Man is not the negotiator; indeed, man has no grounds from which to negotiate.

In the Grip of Grace

Those who find me find life, and the
Lord will be pleased with them.
Proverbs 8:35

JANUARY 19

Grace or God's Goodness

It is through him that we have received grace (God's unmerited favor) and our apostleship to promote obedience to the faith and make disciples for his name's sake among all the nations. And that includes you, called of Jesus Christ and invited (as you are) to belong to him.

Romans 1:5&6 (AMP)

JANUARY 20

Grace or God's Goodness

Grace is used five times in Romans 11:5-6. Even so at this present time, also there is a remnant according to the election of grace. And if by grace, then it is no more works: otherwise grace is no more grace. But if it be works than it is no more "of grace otherwise work is no more work."

JANUARY 21

Grace Upon Grace

Test this question: What if God's only gift to you was his grace to save you.

Would you be content?

You beg <u>him</u> to save the life of your child.

You <u>plead</u> with <u>him</u> to keep your <u>business</u> afloat.

You <u>implore</u> him to remove the cancer from your body.

What if <u>his</u> answer is, "My grace is enough."

JANUARY 22

Grace Upon Grace

Would you be content?

You see from heaven's perspective, grace is enough.

If God did nothing more than save us from hell, could anyone complain? Having been given eternal life, dare we grumble at an aching body? Having been given heavenly riches, dare we bemoan earthly poverty?

If you have eyes to read these words, hand to hold this book, the means to own this volume, he has already given you grace upon grace.

JANUARY 23

Grace

1 Timothy 1:14, Ephesians 2:8-9, Galatians 2:16

The grace of our Lord was poured out on abundantly. It is by grace you have been saved, through faith – and this not from yourselves. It is the gift of God – not by works so that no one observing the law but by faith in Jesus Christ.

JANUARY 24

Grace

Even before I was born God had chosen me to be his, and
called me – what kindness and grace to reveal his Son
within me.
Galatians 1:15-16

JANUARY 25

Grace

He alone is my rock and my salvation; he is my fortress,
I will not be shaken.
Psalm 62:6 (NIV)

JANUARY 26

Faith Is A Gift

For I say through the grace given unto me to every man that
is among you, not to think of himself more highly than he
ought to think: but to think soberly, according as God hath
dealt to every man the measure of faith.
Romans 12:3

JANUARY 27

Faith Is A Gift

Now therefore, (reverently) fear the Lord and serve him in sincerity and in truth; and if it seems evil to you to serve the Lord, choose for yourselves this day whom you will serve, whether the gods which your fathers served on the other side of the river, or the gods of the Amorites, in whose land you dwell, but as for me and my house we will serve the Lord.

Joshua 24:14 & 15 (AMP)

JANUARY 28

Fear Turned Into Faith

Perfect <u>Love</u> cast out fear.

Building up yourselves <u>on your most holy faith</u>!!!
Jude 20

JANUARY 29

Fear Turned Into Faith

For you who <u>fear</u> my name, the son of <u>righteousness</u> will <u>rise</u> with <u>healing</u> in his wings. And you will go <u>free</u>, leaping with <u>joy</u> like calves let out to pasture.
Malachi 4:2 (TLB)

JANUARY 30

Fear Turned Into Faith

Not by might, nor by power, but by my Spirit, say the Lord
Almighty – you will succeed because my Spirit,
though you are few and weak. Amen.
Zechariah 4:6 (TLB)

JANUARY 31

Fear Turned Into Faith

A person is justified by what he does and not faith alone –
the man who look intently into the perfect law that gives
freedom, and continues to do this, not forgetting, what he
had heard, <u>but doing it – he will be blessed</u>.
James 2:24 & James 1:25

(GOLDEN NUGGET)
Faith is a gift that must be developed.

FEBRUARY 1

Living With Christ

Would you like to know him?

For me to live is Christ, and to die is gain.
(Philippians 1:21)

FEBRUARY 2

Living With Christ

Philippians 1:20-23

[20]I eagerly expect and hope that I will in no way be exalted in my body, whether by life or by death.

[21]For me to live is Christ, and to die is gain.

[22]If I am to go on living in the body this will mean fruitful labor for me yet what shall I choose? I do not know!

[23]I desire to depart and be with Christ, which is better by far.

Galatians 2:20

I am crucified with Christ: Nevertheless I live; yet not I, but Christ liveth in me: And the life which I now live in the flesh "I live by faith of the Son of God, who loved me, and gave himself for me.

FEBRUARY 3

Jesus or Nothing, Jesus or No-thing

Jesus or Nothing
Jesus or No-thing

In the Morning

In the Noon-Day

In the Mid-Day (Nighttime)

In the Midnight

FEBRUARY 4

Jesus or Nothing, Jesus or No-thing

You are going to have the light just a little while longer.
Walk while you have the light, before darkness overtakes
you. The man who walks in the dark does not know where is
going. Put your trust in the light while you have it, so that
you may become Sons of Light.
John 15:35-36

FEBRUARY 5

Christ Body Was A Real Body

1. It could be touched

Matthew 28:9
And as they went to tell his disciples, behold, Jesus met them, saying, All hail. And they came and held him by the feet, and worshipped him.

FEBRUARY 6

Christ Body Was A Real Body

2. It had flesh and bones

Luke24:39
Behold my hands and my feet, that it is I myself: handle me, and see; for a spirit hath not flesh and bones as ye see me have.

FEBRUARY 7

Christ Body Was A Real Body

3. It was recognized as the same body not another

John 20:27
Then saith he to Thomas, Reach hither thy finger, and behold my hands; and reach hither thy hand, and thrust it into my side: and be not faithless, but believing.

FEBRUARY 8

Christ Body Was A Real Body

4. It appears that these marks will be visible at his Second Coming

Zechariah 12:10

And I will pour upon the house of David, and upon the inhabitants of Jerusalem, the spirit of grace and of supplications: and they shall look upon me whom they have pierced, and they shall mourn for him, as one mourneth for his only son, and shall be in bitterness for him, as one that is in bitterness for his firstborn.

FEBRUARY 9

Christ Body Was A Real Body

5. It appears that these marks will be visible at his Second Coming

Revelations 1:7

Behold, he cometh with clouds; and every eye shall see him, and they also which pierced him: and all kindreds of the earth shall wail because of him. Even so, Amen.

FEBRUARY 10

Christ Body Was A Real Body

6. It was recognized at different times after the resurrection

Luke 24:41-43

[41]And while they yet believed not for joy, and wondered, he said unto them, Have ye here any meat?

[42]And they gave him a piece of a broiled fish, and of an honeycomb.

[43]And he took it, and did eat before them.

FEBRUARY 11

Christ Body Was A Real Body

7. It was recognized at different times after the resurrection

John 20:16, 20
[16]Jesus saith unto her, Mary. She turned herself, and saith unto him, Rabboni; which is to say, Master.
[20]And when he had so said, he shewed unto them his hand and his side. Then were the disciples glad, when they saw the LORD.

FEBRUARY 12

Christ Body Was A Real Body

8. It was recognized at different times after the resurrection

John 21:7
Therefore that disciple whom Jesus loved saith unto Peter, It is the Lord. Now when Simon Peter heard that it was the Lord, he girt his fisher's coat unto him, (for he was naked,) and did cast himself into the sea.

FEBRUARY 13

Christ Body Was A Real Body

9. He passed through closed doors

John 20:19
Then the same day at evening, being the first day of the week, when the doors were shut where the disciples were assembled for fear of the Jews, came Jesus and stood in the midst, and saith unto them, Peace be unto you.

FEBRUARY 14

Christ Body Was A Real Body

10. He is ALIVE forever more!

Romans 6:9
Knowing that Christ being raised from the dead dieth no more; death hath no more dominion over him.

(Valentine's Day)

FEBRUARY 15

Christ Body Was A Real Body

11. He is ALIVE forever more!

2 Timothy 1:10
But is now made manifest by the appearing of our Saviour
Jesus Christ, who hath abolished death, and hath brought life
and immortality to light through the gospel:

FEBRUARY 16

Christ Body Was A Real Body

12. He is ALIVE forever more!

Revelations 1:18
I am he that liveth, and was dead; and, behold, I am alive for evermore, Amen; and have the keys of hell and of death.

FEBRUARY 17

Jesus Got Up

He is not here, but has risen! Remember how he told you while he was still in Galilee that the son of man must be given over into the hands of sinful men (men whose way or nature is to act in opposition to God) and be crucified and on the third day rise (from death). And they remembered his words.

Luke 24:6-8 (AMP)

FEBRUARY 18

Jesus Got Up

But most of all, thank you Lord Jesus that you got up,
you got up on the third day, after sleeping all night Friday,
and all night Saturday, but on that third day, early one
Sunday morning, you got up with all your might,
With all power in your hands.

Thank you God for your glorious plan,
To give to us life through your son, an excellent man,
Who took a stand for the people of this great land.

FEBRUARY 19

Wake Up

But we speak the wisdom of God in a mystery, even the hidden wisdom, which God ordained before the world unto our glory.
1 Corinthians 2:7

(Washington's Birthday)

FEBRUARY 20

Wake Up

When you wake up in the morning what is the first
Thing that you do?
Do you give thanks?
And who do you give it to?

Do you ask yourself what woke you up this day?
Was it your alarm clock?
Or was it your dog's bark?

Do you just get up out of bed?
Without anything going through your head?

FEBRUARY 21

Wake Up

Or do you think about the things that were said,
How your life is being led,
And your mind, body, and soul being fed?

Ask yourself again who woke me up?
Then tell yourself that God did it, yup.

It was not the alarm clock,
the dog's bark,
It was God himself with his mystical spark.

FEBRUARY 22

Rise My Child

Little children let us stop just saying we love people; let us really love them, and show it by our actions. Then, we will know for sure by our actions, that we are on God's side and our consciences will be clear, even when we stand before the Lord.

1 John 3:18-19 (TLB)

FEBRUARY 23

Rise My Child

Rise my child
Rise to the occasion
It may be short or it may be long.
Rise because you do not want to prolong.

Rise I said, rise my child.
You are a child today
Therefore be happy regardless what anyone may say.

Rise my child, rise.
I can see love in your eyes,
and peace in your heart.

Rise, rise to the top
My little child, please do not stop.
Look up and rise,
In order to see what lies.

Rise my child, rise.
You can conquer your dreams
No matter how difficult it seems.

FEBRUARY 24

Rise My Child

Therefore, rise, I said rise,
To see what lies.
Beyond all your tries and cries.

Rise my child, rise.
Rise like the sun
Your life has just begun.
And your battle is already won.

Rise my child, rise my little child,
Rise to it all, one thing for sure it's your call.

Rise, rise my little child,
You decide if you fall,
That it will be a ball.

Get up and dust yourself off,
Try and try again.
Rise, rise my child.

Rise like the sun,
Your life has just begun
Rise above it all,
Remember it is your call,
So rise, rise, rise my little child.

FEBRUARY 25

It's A Wonder

The secret things belong unto the Lord our God; but those things which are revealed belong unto us and to our children forever, that we may do all the words of this law.
Deuteronomy 29:29

FEBRUARY 26

It's A Wonder

Do you ever wonder about the holy bible story
Since you know that there is heaven's glory.

Do you ever wonder about heaven and earth
And how Mary gave birth.

Do you ever wonder how the clouds darken over you
But the sun shines and comes right through.

Do you ever wonder how the birds fly
And you still have peace even when you cry.

Do you ever wonder how it rains over there
But where you live the rain does not come near.

Do you ever wonder how the seasons change
When you don't see anyone here that can rearrange.

FEBRUARY 27

It's A Wonder

Do you ever wonder how the night turns into day
When you lay.

Do you ever wonder who gave you sight
You are able to see even in the night.

Do you ever wonder how you can hear
When you are far away and you don't see anyone near.
Do you ever wonder how foxes live in the wild
And women give birth to a child.

FEBRUARY 28

It's A Wonder

*Do you ever wonder how water is made
When there is a drought and your water bill is still not paid.*

*Do you ever wonder about the waves in the ocean
How the waves still keep motion.*

*Do you ever wonder how when in thunders
You know where and what to get under.*

MARCH 1

It's A Wonder

*Do you ever wonder how you write a check and know that
you don't have any funds
But you still write it for a certain amount of sum.*

*Do you ever wonder how you won the case
When you know that there was a lot of time that you faced.*

*Do you ever wonder how the wind blows
And the river flows.*

*Do you ever wonder how you get fired
And then turn around and get hired.*

MARCH 2

It's A Wonder

Do you ever wonder how you got a position
That you applied
But you knew that you were not qualified.
Do you ever wonder how you give your last dime
And then you look in your mailbox and see a check that
was right on time.

Do you ever wonder how you can pray
When you are not having a pleasant day.

Do you ever wonder how your boss tells you no
But then later you ask it changes to a go.

It's A Wonder

Do you ever wonder how you get disapproved
And then go somewhere else and get approved.

Do you ever wonder how you breathe
When the clean air seems to leave.

Do you ever wonder how we have grace
When you have never seen his face.

MARCH 4

It's A Wonder

Lord you have been our dwelling place and our refuge in all generations (says Moses). Before the mountains were brought forth or ever you had formed and given birth to the earth and world, even from everlasting to everlasting you are God.

Psalm 90:1-2 (AMP)

MARCH 5

Lord Give Me A Song

He touched me, oh he touched me and oh the joy that fill my soul, something happened and now I know he touched me and made me whole.

Jesus, Jesus, there is just something about that name Master Savior Jesus – like the fragrance after the rain.

Oh Jesus, Jesus, Jesus, let all heaven and earth proclaim, Kings and kingdoms will all past away but there's something about that name.

Talk with each other much about the Lord, quoting psalms and hymns and singing sacred songs, making music in your hearts to the Lord. Always give thanks for everything to our God and Father in the name of our Lord Jesus Christ. Honor Christ by submitting to each other.
Ephesians 5:19-21 (TLB)

MARCH 6

Lord Give Me A Song

Give me a song that sticks close to my heart
Lord, I know whatever you give me it will never part.

I know you will give me a song that will give you praise,
For the rest of my days.

Give me a song that lifts you higher
A beautiful song that I can sing out loud in the shower,
Regardless of the day or the hour.

Give me a song that dwells in me
For you to see
And allows me to know how you be.

Lord Give Me A Song

Give me a song that I can praise you all day long,
Even to the crack of dawn.

Give me a song that tells your story
It will make me sing glory.

Give me a song that will give me strength
And magnifies your name to every length.

Give me a song that I can sing all day long
Since I know that you, the one and only true and
Wise God, sits on the throne.

MARCH 8

Choice

For a <u>shepherd comes through</u> the gate. The <u>gatekeeper</u> opens the gate for him and the sheep <u>hear</u> his <u>voice</u> and come to him; and he calls his own sheep by name and lead them out. He walks ahead of them and they follow him, for they <u>recognize</u> his <u>voice</u>. They won't <u>follow</u> a <u>stranger</u> but will <u>run</u> from <u>him</u>, for they don't <u>recognize</u> his <u>voice</u>.
John 10:2-5 (TLB)

MARCH 9

<u>Choice</u>

For eternal life is the gift of God.
For eternal death is the result of no God.

For man has a choice,
So please listen for his voice.

For his voice is clear,
And always near.

For his love is unconditional
However, definitely intentional.

MARCH 10

Choice

For your life,
He paid the price.

So that you and I can have life,
And life more abundantly.

For man has a choice,
When he hears his voice.

So therefore rejoice with your choice,
When you hear his awesome voice.

MARCH 11

Different Choices

<u>Jesus said</u> for whoever wants to save his life will lose it, but whoever loses his life for me will save it. What good is it for a man to gain the whole world, and yet lose or forfeit his very self (soul)?

Luke 9:24-25 (NIV)

(Daylight Savings Time Begins)

MARCH 12

Different Choices

I know that we don't talk the way we use to,
We don't go out together the way we use to,
We don't go to clubs.

I guess we have chosen different routes,
Without having any doubts,
Even when choosing our spouse.

You invite me to clubs,
You invite me to cabarets,
You invite me to see strippers.

These are the places and choices you have made.
But I will not criticize your choices,
Because we have chose different routes.

Instead of me criticizing your choices,
I pray for you because I love you.
Despite your choices, who am I to judge?

Different Choices

I have made the choice to choose Christ for my life.
This is so nice.

I ask you to come to church,
I ask you come to bible study,
I ask you to come to prayer service,
I ask you to come to plays,
I ask you come together as sisters so that we can pray.
Although we have chose different roads,
Life is still a choice,
And you have a voice.

Different Choices

A voice to choose,
So that you will not lose.

So what road will you choose?
To serve Christ or not?
If not you will lose a lot!

You will lose your soul,
So what is your goal?
To gain the world and lose your soul?

MARCH 15

To Have Christ

To live is to have Christ.
Ooh, this is so nice.

To die is to gain.
But we must suffer his pain.

Not knowing Christ is having no light.
There is pure darkness that will sustain the night.

When we carry the cross with him,
We will not be lost,
Because one thing for sure he is the boss.

You can have the Father and Christ for a simple price.
Just repent your sins and confess that Jesus is Lord,
And get on board, so that we can be one body
in Christ on one accord.

MARCH 16

Know

But this is the covenant of Israel: After those days, says them, and on their hearts will I write it: And I will be their God, and they will be my people. And they will no more teach each man his neighbor and each man his brother, saying, know the Lord, for they will all know me (recognize, understand and be acquainted with me), from the least of them to the greatest, says the Lord. For I will forgive their iniquity, and I will (seriously) remember their sin no more.

Jeremiah 31:33-34 (AMP)

MARCH 17

<u>Know</u>

Knowing is to know.
To know is to know who you are.

You are who you are.
Because you know every fiber of your being.

Therefore to know is to love.
To love is to know.
To know is to know yourself.

Knowing yourself is to know Jesus.
For man was created in his image,
And to know Jesus is to know peace.

Peace is to know,
And to have peace
Is to know Jesus, the Prince of Peace.

MARCH 18

Knowledge

Job 37:16
Do you know how the clouds hang poised, those wonders of him who is perfect in **knowledge**?

MARCH 19

Knowledge

Job 38:2
"Who is this that darkens my counsel with words without knowledge?

MARCH 20

Knowledge

Job 42:3

You asked, 'Who is this that obscures my counsel without **knowledge**?' Surely I spoke of things I did not understand, things too wonderful for me to know.

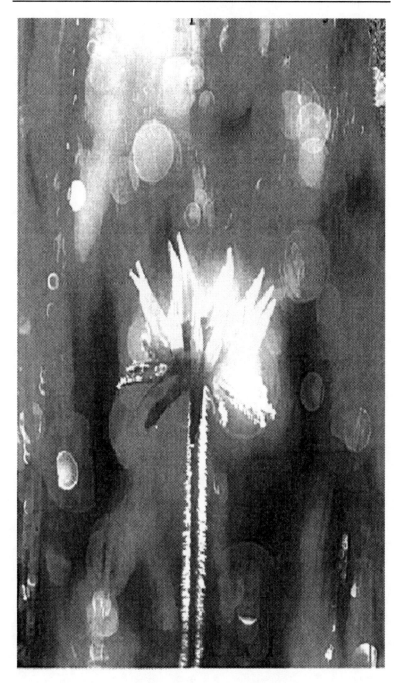

MARCH 21

Knowledge

Psalm 19:2
Day after day they pour forth speech; night after night they display **knowledge**.

(First Day of Spring)

MARCH 22

Knowledge

Psalm 73:11
They say, "How can God know? Does the Most High have **knowledge**?"

MARCH 23

Knowledge

Psalm 94:10
Does he who disciplines nations not punish? Does he who teaches man lack **knowledge**?

MARCH 24

Knowledge

Psalm 119:66
Teach me **knowledge** and good judgment, for I believe in your commands.

MARCH 25

Knowledge

Psalm 139:6
Such **knowledge** is too wonderful for me, too lofty for me to attain.

MARCH 26

Knowledge

Proverbs 1:4
For giving prudence to the simple, **knowledge** and discretion to the young.

MARCH 27

Knowledge

Proverbs 1:7
The fear of the LORD is the beginning of **knowledge**, but fools [The Hebrew words rendered fool in Proverbs, and often elsewhere in the Old Testament, denote one who is morally deficient.] despise wisdom and discipline.

MARCH 28

Knowledge

Genesis 2:9

And the LORD God made all kinds of trees grow out of the ground—trees that were pleasing to the eye and good for food. In the middle of the garden were the tree of life and the tree of the **knowledge** of good and evil.

MARCH 29

Knowledge

Genesis 2:17
But you must not eat from the tree of the **knowledge** of good and evil, for when you eat of it you will surely die."

MARCH 30

Knowledge

Exodus 31:3
And I have filled him with the Spirit of God, with skill, ability and **knowledge** in all kinds of crafts.

MARCH 31

Knowledge

Exodus 35:31
And he has filled him with the Spirit of God, with skill, ability and **knowledge** in all kinds of crafts.

APRIL 1

Knowledge

Numbers 24:16
The oracle of one who hears the words of God, who has **knowledge** from the Most High, who sees a vision from the Almighty, who falls prostrate, and whose eyes are opened:

APRIL 2

Knowledge

1 Kings 2:32
The LORD will repay him for the blood he shed, because without the **knowledge** of my father David he attacked two men and killed them with the sword. Both of them—Abner son of Ner, commander of Israel's army, and Amasa son of Jether, commander of Judah's army—were better men and more upright than he.

APRIL 3

Knowledge

2 Chronicles 1:10
Give me wisdom and **knowledge,** that I may lead this people, for who is able to govern this great people of yours?"
(First Day of Passover)

APRIL 4

Knowledge

2 Chronicles 1:11
God said to Solomon, "Since this is your heart's desire and you have not asked for wealth, riches or honor, nor for the death of your enemies, and since you have not asked for a long life but for wisdom and **knowledge** to govern my people over whom I have made you king,

Knowledge

2 Chronicles 1:12
Therefore wisdom and **knowledge** will be given you. And I will also give you wealth, riches and honor, such as no king who was before you ever had and none after you will have."

APRIL 6

Knowledge

Job 21:22
"Can anyone teach **knowledge** to God, since he judges even the highest?

(Good Friday)

APRIL 7

Knowledge

Job 34:35
'Job speaks without **knowledge**; his words lack insight.'

APRIL 8

Knowledge

Job 35:16
So Job opens his mouth with empty talk; without **knowledge** he multiplies words."

(Easter)

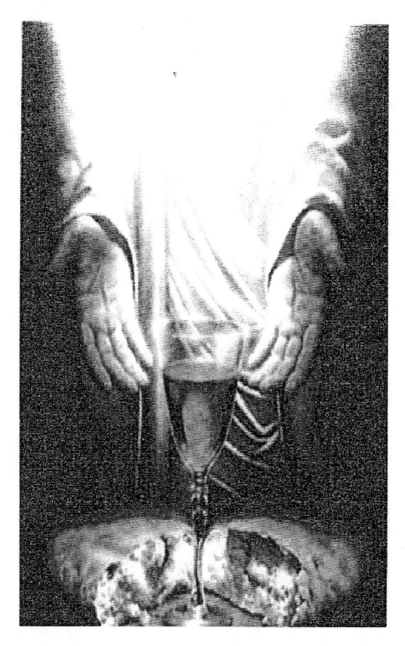

APRIL 9

Knowledge

Job 36:3
I get my **knowledge** from afar; I will ascribe justice to my Maker.

APRIL 10

Knowledge

Job 36:4
Be assured that my words are not false; one perfect in
knowledge is with you.
(Last Day of Passover)

APRIL 11

Knowledge

Job 36:12
But if they do not listen, they will perish by the sword [Or will cross the River] and die without **knowledge**.

APRIL 12

Am I Alone?

On one cloudy day, I felt so alone.
I looked around the room to see who was there.
As I sat quietly I heard a voice whisper I am here.
I am here because I care.

APRIL 13

<u>Am I Alone?</u>

I am your friend,
I am here for you,
No matter how blue.

Your life may be gloom,
Situation doomed,
But at the cross there is room.

APRIL 14

Am I Alone?

Room for you and many more,
No matter how much burdens you may bore,
Remember I am your core.

APRIL 15

Am I Alone?

The core of your inner most being,
The source of your life,
I am the way the truth and life.

The life that you can have eternally,
When you place nothing above me,
For I am the one who allows you to see,
The one that enables you to be.

APRIL 16

Am I Alone?

So you are not alone,
Even when you feel like you are stoned,
With your body cold to the bone.

Remember I dwell inside,
Even when you try to hide,
I am on your side.

I speak in a soft tone,
But remember you are never alone.

APRIL 17

A True Friend

Two are better than one; because they have a good reward for their labor. For if they fall, the one will lift up his fellow: but woe to him that is alone when he falleth; for he hath not another to help him up. Again, if two lie together, they have heat: but how can one be warm alone? And if one prevail against him, two shall withstand him; and a threefold cord is not quickly broken. Amen

Ecclesiastes 4:9-12

A True Friend

Everybody say that they are a friend
but are they really a friend?

A friend is loves you
and doesn't use you.

A friend shows support
without abort.

APRIL 19

A True Friend

*A friend is with you through ups and downs
even when others are no where to be found.*

*A friend will listen to your cry
while others simply leave and say bye.*

*A friend is someone who cares
and they also shares.*

*A friend does not turn their back
when they see that you lack.*

APRIL 20

A True Friend

*A friend holds you
when others scold you.*

*A friend is there
when no one else seems to care.*

*A friend tells you your faults
to help change your thoughts.*

APRIL 21

A True Friend

*A friend is consistent
and not distant.*

*A friend encourages
when others show discourage.*

*A friend may say that they are true
but they are not there for all you do.*

*A friend is nice
but no friend is as good as Christ.*

APRIL 22

Friend

Psalm 119:63
I am a **friend** to all who fear you, to all who follow your precepts.

Psalm 122:8
For the sake of my brothers and **friend**s, I will say, "Peace be within you."

APRIL 23

Friend

Proverbs 12:26
A righteous man is cautious in **friend**ship, [Or man is a guide to his neighbor] but the way of the wicked leads them astray.

Proverbs 14:20
The poor are shunned even by their neighbors, but the rich have many **friend**s.

APRIL 24

Friend

Proverbs 16:28
A perverse man stirs up dissension, and a gossip separates close **friends.**

Proverbs 17:9
He who covers over an offense promotes love, but whoever repeats the matter separates close **friends.**

APRIL 25

Friend

Proverbs 17:17
A **friend** loves at all times, and a brother is born for adversity.

Proverbs 18:24
A man of many companions may come to ruin, but there is a **friend** who sticks closer than a brother.

APRIL 26

Friend

Proverbs 19:4
Wealth brings many **friend**s, but a poor man's **friend** deserts him.

Proverbs 19:6
Many curry favor with a ruler, and everyone is the **friend** of a man who gives gifts.

APRIL 27

Friend

Proverbs 19:7
A poor man is shunned by all his relatives— how much more do his **friend**s avoid him! Though he pursues them with pleading, they are nowhere to be found. [The meaning of the Hebrew for this sentence is uncertain.]

APRIL 28

Friend

Proverbs 22:11
He who loves a pure heart and whose speech is gracious will have the king for his **friend**.

Proverbs 22:24
Do not make **friend**s with a hot-tempered man, do not associate with one easily angered,

APRIL 29

Friend

Proverbs 27:6
Wounds from a **friend** can be trusted, but an enemy multiplies kisses.

Proverbs 27:9
Perfume and incense bring joy to the heart, and the pleasantness of one's **friend** springs from his earnest counsel.

APRIL 30

Friend

Proverbs 27:10
Do not forsake your **friend** and the **friend** of your father, and do not go to your brother's house when disaster strikes you— better a neighbor nearby than a brother far away.

Peace Be Still

I am leaving you with a gift – peace of mind and heart! And the peace I give isn't fragile like the <u>peace</u> the world gives. So don't be troubled or afraid. Remember what I told you I am going away, but I will come back to you again. If you really love me, you will be very happy for me, for now I can go to the Father, <u>who is</u> greater <u>than I am</u>.

John 14:27-28 (TLB)

<u>Peace Be Still</u>

Hey there,
Can we talk a moment?
Can you tell me something?

By the way what is your intention?
Not to mention, you have caused so much tension.
The tension has caused you to try everything in the world!

Peace Be Still

You tried different medicines,
You tried the doctor,
You tried herbal remedies,
You tried exercising,
You tried resting,
But all these things have seemed to fail.

Can I ask you something?
Have you tried Jesus?
He is the only one that can please us,
As he leads us.

Peace Be Still

Well, she answered, no I haven't tried him but I will.
If you will, I promise you he will.
His will is his Father's will.
Do his will, then girl, you will be able to chill.
Because he said, PEACE BE STILL.

Then I thought to myself and said girl,
If God can still the waters,
Girl, we must obey his orders.
So, he said, peace be still, and know that I am God.

Why Wait

Also I heard the voice of the Lord saying, whom shall I send, and who will go for us. Then said I, here am I, send me. And he said, go, and tell this people, hear ye indeed, but understand not; and see indeed, but perceive not.
Isaiah 6:8-9

Why Wait

You can travel around the world
see the most beautiful places
and try foods that have a special taste.

You can travel to an island,
a desert, a mountain,
or even a place that looks like a fountain.

Why Wait

You can travel by plane
You can get there by train.

You can travel by bus,
Or get there by car
Even if the place is far.

You can travel by van
Or by a caravan.

MAY 8

Why Wait

You can travel wherever you want to go
As long as you have the dough.

For it is God that has the say so
That allows you to go to the places that you know and don't
know.
So trust in God in your travel and go.

It Does Not Matter

For we <u>through,</u> the Spirit wait for the hope of righteousness
by faith.
Galatians 5:5

(For we walk by faith, not by sight:)
2 Corinthians 5:7

MAY 10

It Does Not Matter

It does not matter what you are going through,
The times may be rough,
and you are carrying around a lot of stuff.

It does not matter what you are going through,
All you need to do is unload the stuff,
Because haven't you had enough.

It Does Not Matter

It does not matter what you are going through,
Some days you may feel weary,
And some days you may be merry,
But however you feel, just know that Jesus will carry.

MAY 12

It Does Not Matter

It does not matter what you are going through,
Continue to cry and pray all night,
Keep up the good fight,
Because we know that Jesus is light.

MAY 13

It Does Not Matter

It does not matter what you are going through,
It does not matter how blue,
It does not matter how true,
All that matter is that you make it through.

(Mother's Day)

MAY 14

Change Your Attitude

But how is it to your credit if you receive a beating for doing wrong and endure it? But if you suffer for doing good and endure it, this is commendable before God. To this you were called, because Christ suffered for you leaving you and example, that you should follow in his steps.
1 Peter 2:20-21 (NIV)

MAY 15

Change Your Attitude

Let's change our attitude,
So that we can show gratitude.

Let's change our attitude,
This can help our latitude.

Let's change our attitude,
It will determine your altitude.

Let's change our attitude,
Turn negatives
Into positives.

MAY 16

Change Your Attitude

Let's change our attitude,
Don't show aggravation
Show appreciation.

Let's change our attitude,
Don't keep committing sin
Since you will not win.

Change Your Attitude

Let's change our attitude,
A failure is a lesson learned
So that the success can be earned.

Let's change our attitude,
Show love for your enemies
Even though they do not deserve it.
Through God's grace he reserved it.

Help the Needy

But if someone who supposed to be a Christian has money enough to live well, and sees a brother in need, and won't help him – how can God's love be within him?
1 John 3:17 (TLB)

Help the Needy

We need to help the poor
They shouldn't hunger anymore.

We need to pray for the people that are ill
And help them pay their doctor's bill.

We need to help the needy
And stop being so greedy.

We need to provide shelter
So that our people can live better.

1

MAY 20

<u>Help the Needy</u>

We need to show them how to pray
And let them know that God's love will stay.

So why don't we share
To show the less fortunate that we care.

Why do we continue to talk
Without showing others how to walk.

Why do we keep giving lip
Without providing any script.

Why do we think we are superior
When actually no one is inferior.

Why don't we tell the needy about God
And simply tell them to ask him for their daily bread
So that they can be spiritually fed and led.

MAY 21

A Heart Like His

When anxiety was great within me, your consolation brought joy to my soul. I call as my heart grows fain; lead me to the rock that is higher than I. I am troubled; O Lord come to my aid! – "Take heart, son; your sins are forgiven." "Take heart, daughter, he said your faith has healed you."
Ezekiel 11:19-20 (NIV)

MAY 22

A Heart Like Yours (Written by Cece Winans)

I tried to reach out for <u>you</u> but I fall
Sometimes you seem so close,
And yet so far
Oh I need another chance
I need to know <u>your</u> mercy
Just give me the strength,
To change within

I know I'm not all that I can be
My weakness seems to get the best of me
But as long as you are here,
I know that I will make it
Every step along the way
Please hear my prayer

A heart like yours, is my desire
A heart like yours
Is what I'm searching for
Full of compassion,
Nothing wrong within
Please hear me Lord,
Give me an ear like yours

So much grace, so much kindness
So much faith, forever true
Strong as the wind, soft as the shadows
If just once, I could be like <u>you.</u>

A heart like yours is my desire!

MAY 23

Love from the Heart of God
(Written by Bishop D. Downing)

If everything that has ever been written about love was gathered together and laid side-by-side, the line would probably encircle the globe. Human writers and artists have produced many wonderful and sublime expressions of love through the ages, but even the greatest of them do not equal the love book given by God himself. The Bible, still the number one best seller throughout the world, is the greatest love story ever told: the story of God's eternal love affair with mankind.

From the very first page the love of God shines forth, so vast and deep, so tender and complete that it reaches beyond human wisdom, knowledge, and understanding. God's love cuts through the mind, the spirit, and the flesh, reaching into the secret, precious inner self – the hidden man of the heart – where his treasures are kept. God's love for us is evident throughout the Scriptures not only in what he says, but also in what he does. Consider these words from Jeremiah: The Lord hath appeared of old unto me, saying yea, I have loved thee with an everlasting love; therefore with loving kindness have I drawn thee (Jeremiah 31:3).

Name of Book – Hidden Treasures of the Heart, Written by
Bishop Donald Downing

MAY 24

Turning Wrongs Into Rights

Do what is right; then if men speak against you, calling you evil names they will become ashamed of themselves for falsely accusing you when you have only done what is good.
1 Peter 3:16 (TLB)

MAY 25

Turning Wrongs Into Rights

When you do wrong
Christ can make your wrongs right.

When you create a mess
Christ will still bless.

When you lie
Christ will still remain nigh.

When you refuse to love
The heavens will open up from above.

When you try to hide
God is still on your side.

MAY 26

Turning Wrongs Into Rights

When you sin
Jesus will still let you in.

When you are sad
God will still be glad.

When you use dope
Jesus will give you hope.

When you are in trouble
God will be there on the double.

When human judgments fail
God's justice will prevail.

MAY 27

A Righteous Heart Is the Fountain of Beauty

The Word became flesh and made his dwelling among us.
We have seen his glory, the glory of the One and Only, who
came from the Father, full of grace and truth.
John 1:14 (NIV)

MAY 28

A Righteous Heart Is the Fountain of Beauty

The tabernacle in the wilderness was a tent where the glory of God dwelt the structure was made of badger skins and was plain on the outside. But inside it was exquisitely beautiful (Exodus 25-27).

(Memorial Day)

MAY 29

A Righteous Heart Is the Fountain of Beauty

We can compare the tabernacle with Jesus' human form. John said, "the Word became flesh and dwelt among us (John 1:14). The word dwelt means he "pitched his tent with us," the same word that ancient Greek versions of the Old Testament used for the tabernacle. Jesus looked like an ordinary man: He had "no beauty that we should desire him" (Isaiah 53:2). No one gave him a second look. Yet John "behold his glory, the glory of God himself." Occasionally, the tent flap was lifted and he caught a glimpse of Jesus inner beauty and majesty.

MAY 30

A Righteous Heart Is the Fountain of Beauty

We are tabernacles too, made of skin made to contain God's Spirit. Most of us are very plain, not like the made-up actors we see in the movies or the air-brushed models we view in the ads. But God is even now-at this moment-in the process of making vs. radiantly beautiful within.

MAY 31

A Righteous Heart Is the Fountain of Beauty

We may be very plain and ordinary on the outside-but as we allow God's Spirit to work within us, the beauty of God's indwelling presence will shine from our faces. So, is the world seeing Jesus in you?

By David Riper, Writer for the Our Daily Bread

JUNE 1

Inner Beauty

"Let the beauty of Jesus been seen in me, All his wonderful passion and purity; O thou Spirit divine, all my nature refine till the beauty of Jesus be seen in me" (quoted by Orsborn, Our Daily Bread).

JUNE 2

Letter to God: Can You Do It For Me?

I can do all things through Christ which strengtheneth me.
Philippians 4:13

JUNE 3

Letter to God: Can You Do It for Me?

Hi God,

It's me, you know me,
It's me again Lord,
I need you today,
I have decided that I need you everyday,
and in every way.

Lord, there have been times
That you know that I did not have a dime,
But I held on to my faith so that I would not commit a crime.

Lord, can you bless me?
Before the law arrest me,
Can you direct me?
Before I wreck me.

JUNE 4

Letter to God: Can You Do It For Me?

Lord, can you shape me?
Mold me?
Hold me?
Console me?
Use me?
Whatever it is Lord that I need, can you give it to me?

JUNE 5

Letter to God: Can You Do It For Me?

Give it to me Lord please.
I am on my bending knees.
Master, as you can see I am in need, yes indeed.

I know Lord I call on your name,
But in your Word you always stay the same,
And I want you to know that you are my fame, Because you
sent your son Jesus whom I will always claim.

Theme: Prayer

Prayer when surrounded by trouble or wickedness. God is our only real source of safety.

Prayer is our best help when trials come our way because it keeps us in communion with God.

Prayer

Seek the Lord and his strength, seek his face continually, and say ye, save us, O God of our salvation, and gather us together, and deliver us from the heathen, that we may give thanks to thy holy name, and glory in thy praise.
1 Chronicles 16:11, 35

JUNE 8

Prayer

Nevertheless we made our prayer unto our God, and set a
watch against the day and night because of them.
Nehemiah 4:9

JUNE 9

Prayer

When thou saidist, seek ye my face: my heart said unto thee, thy face, Lord will I seek.
Psalm 27:8

JUNE 10

Prayer

Glory ye in his holy name; let the heart of them rejoice that
seek the Lord. Seek the Lord and his strength:
seek his face forevermore.
Psalm 105:34
Amen!

JUNE 11

Prayer

For out of the abundance of the heart the mouth speaketh. A good man bringeth forth good things and an evil man bringeth forth evil things.
Matthew 12:34, 35

JUNE 12

Prayer

Ye have not chosen me, but I have chosen you and ordained
you, that he should go and bring forth fruit and that your
fruit should remain.
John 15:6

JUNE 13

Prayer

"But the natural man received not the things of the Spirit of God: For they are foolishness unto him."
1 Corinthians 2:14

"And we know that all things work together for good to them that love God."
Romans 8:28

"God wants to use us as He used his own Son."

JUNE 14

Pray In Secret

He who dwells in the secret place of the most high shall remain stable and fixed under the shadow of the Almighty (whose power no foe can withstand). I will say of the Lord, he is my refuge and my fortress, my God; on him I lean and rely, and in him I confidently trust! Amen
Psalm 91:1-2 (AMP)

<u>Pray in Secret</u>

*Oh, my Lord, help me to shut the door
and kneel down on the floor.
Seek ye Lord,
It is you that I am looking for.*

*Help me Lord to set everything else aside,
Because with you is where I want to abide.*

*Oh, my Lord, help me to go into a secret place to pray,
For it is by your grace that I am able to stay.*

*Help me to pray, Oh Lord!
It is your mercy that keeps me.
And your goodness that set me free.*

JUNE 16

Pray in Secret

Oh, my Lord, I know whatever I pray in secret
You will reveal it and make sure that I receive it.

Help me to pray and say thanks,
Thanks for all you have done
It was by your grace through faith that I awoke to see the sun.

JUNE 17

Pray in Secret

Oh, my Lord, help me to pray in secret
Because I am weak and
I need to hear you speak
For it is you that I seek
Each day in every week.

So Lord, I pray in the most high secret place
So that one day I can see your beautiful face
When I finally leave this race.

(Father's Day)

JUNE 18

<u>Prayer Changes Things</u>

But thou when thou prayest enter into thy closet and when thou has shut thy door, pray to thy father which seeth in secret shall reward thee openly. But not ye therefore like unto them: for your father knoweth what things ye have need of, before ye ask him. Amen

Matthew 6:6, 8

JUNE 19

Prayer Changes Things

When you start your day,
You should pray,
Prayer changes things.

Pray for wisdom
When your day is dismal,
Prayer changes things.

When you pray,
The demons will not stay,
When you pray,
Understanding will come your way.

Pray for strength,
When you are weak,
And trying to climb that peak.

JUNE 20

Prayer Changes Things

When you pray,
The enemies will fall,
When you hear God's call.

Pray that you can love,
Love your brethren as you love yourself,
Because we all know that God loves us more than we love
ourselves.

JUNE 21

Prayer Changes Things

When you pray,
Pray not to be rich in possessions,
Pray not to be poor in heart,
Pray so that you will not fall apart.

Pray not to be wealthy,
Pray not to live in poverty,
But pray to share,
So that the people will know that you care.

(First Day of Summer)

JUNE 22

Prayer Changes Things

When you pray,
Do not just pray for you,
Pray for others too.

Pray, pray, pray,
Remember prayer changes things.

JUNE 23

Jesus Loves You

As the father has loved me, so have I loved you. Now remain in my love. If you obey my commands, you will remain in my love, just as I have obeyed my father's commands and remain in his love. I have told you this so that my joy may be in you and that your joy may be complete. My command is this: Love each other as I have loved you.
John 15:9-12 (NIV)

JUNE 24

Jesus Loves You

I know that you are hurting
But just hold on.
It won't be long
Put your trust in God and be strong.

I know that your friends don't treat you right
So just hold on.
The bible says that weeping may endure for a night but joy
comes in the morning light.

JUNE 25

Jesus Loves You

*I know that people don't like you because of your
possessions.
But why should you care
when Jesus is the only one that is just and fair.*

*I know that people talk about you
but you don't know why and don't have a clue,
however just remember they talked about Jesus too.*

JUNE 26

Jesus Loves You

*I know that people hate
but you should pray for them,
before it's too late
for them to enter into heaven's gate.*

*I know that you don't feel loved
just know that you are loved
from the Precious Lamb that sits above.*

JUNE 27

Love For Your Enemies

*All who listen to my instructions and follow them are wise,
like a man who builds his house on solid rock.*
Matthew 7:24 (TLB)

JUNE 28

Love For Your Enemies

The fear of the Lord is the beginning of knowledge, but fools despise wisdom and discipline.
Proverbs 1:7 (NIV)

JUNE 29

Love For Your Enemies

Do what is right, then if men speak against you, calling you evil names, they will become ashamed of themselves for falsely accusing you when you have only done what is good.
1 Peter 3:16 (TLB)

JUNE 30

Love For Your Enemies

Be strong and courageous. Do not be afraid or terrified because of them, for the Lord your God goes with you; he will never leave you or forsake you.
Deuteronomy 31:6 (NIV)

JULY 1

<u>Love For Your Enemies</u>

The Lord himself goes before you and will be with you; he will never leave you nor forsake you. Do not be afraid; do not be discouraged.
Deuteronomy 31:8 (NIV)

You prepared a meal for me in front of my enemies.
Psalm 23:5

Love

Numbers 14:18
'The LORD is slow to anger, abounding in **love** and forgiving sin and rebellion. Yet he does not leave the guilty unpunished; he punishes the children for the sin of the fathers to the third and fourth generation.'

Deuteronomy 6:1
[*Love the LORD Your God*] These are the commands, decrees and laws the LORD your God directed me to teach you to observe in the land that you are crossing the Jordan to possess,

Love

Deuteronomy 6:5
Love the LORD your God with all your heart and with all your soul and with all your strength.

Deuteronomy 7:9
Know therefore that the LORD your God is God; he is the faithful God, keeping his covenant of **love** to a thousand generations of those who **love** him and keep his commands.

Love

Deuteronomy 7:12
If you pay attention to these laws and are careful to follow them, then the LORD your God will keep his covenant of **love** with you, as he swore to your forefathers.
(Independence Day)

Love

Deuteronomy 30:6
The LORD your God will circumcise your hearts and the hearts of your descendants, so that you may **love** him with all your heart and with all your soul, and live.

Deuteronomy 30:16
For I command you today to **love** the LORD your God, to walk in his ways, and to keep his commands, decrees and laws; then you will live and increase, and the LORD your God will bless you in the land you are entering to possess.

JULY 6

Love

Psalm 109:21
But you, O Sovereign LORD, deal well with me for your name's sake; out of the goodness of your **love**, deliver me.

Psalm 109:26
Help me, O LORD my God; save me in accordance with your **love**.

Psalm 115:1
Not to us, O LORD, not to us but to your name be the glory, because of your **love** and faithfulness.

Love

Psalm 116:1
I **love** the LORD, for he heard my voice; he heard my cry for mercy.

Psalm 117:2
For great is his **love** toward us, and the faithfulness of the LORD endures forever. Praise the LORD. [Hebrew Hallelu Yah]

Psalm 118:1
Give thanks to the LORD, for he is good; his **love** endures forever.

Psalm 118:2
Let Israel say: "His **love** endures forever."

Dwell: God "Dwelling in the Light"

Who only hath <u>immortality</u>, dwelling in the Light which no
man hath seen, nor can see: to whom be honor and power
everlasting. Amen
1 Timothy 6:16

Who alone is <u>immortal</u> and lives in unapproachable light,
who no one has seen or can see. To him be honor and might
forever. Amen
1 Timothy 6:16 (NIV)

Dwell: God "Dwelling in the Light"

Who alone can never die, who <u>lives in light</u> so terrible that no human being can approach Him. No mere man has ever seen Him, nor ever will. Unto Him be honor and everlasting power and dominion forever and ever. Amen
1 Timothy 6:16 (TLB)

JULY 10

Dwell: God "Dwelling in the Light"

God is Light

1 John 1:1-3 (NIV)

[1]That which was from the beginning, which we heard, which we have seen with our eyes, which we have looked at and our hands have touched – this we proclaim concerning the Word of Life.

[2]The life appeared; we have seen it and testify to it, and we proclaim to you Eternal life, which was with father and appeared to us.

[3]We proclaim to you what we have seen and heard so that you also may fellowship with us. And our fellowship is with the Father and his Son, Jesus Christ. We write this to make our joy complete.

JULY 11

<u>Do You Know God's Dwelling?</u>

[1]Lord, who shall abide in thy tabernacle? Who shall dwell in
thy holy hill?
[2]He that walketh uprightly, and worketh righteousness, and
speaketh the truth in his heart.
Psalm15:1-2

The Throne Room

"Only in the throne will I be greater than thou."
Genesis 41:40

Before me was a great multitude that no one could count, from every nation, tribe, people & language, standing before the throne … they cried out with a loud voice: Salvation belongs to our God, who sits on the throne and to the Lamb… Praise and glory & wisdom and thanks and honor and power and strength be to our God forever and ever. Amen!
Revelations 7:9-10, 12

JULY 13

Honor God and He Will Honor You

In Psalm 132: Here we see that David want to find a special place where he could rest the ark of the covenant. David was very restless because he wanted to build a place to house the ark other than a tent. As we all know David's son, Solomon, was the one to build the temple but in Solomon's Father David he was the one who had the plan of where the dwelling place should be.

I have a question: Are you happy where you are in God?

We all should be restless or uncomfortable until we complete what the Master started in us. Don't get weary in well doing.

JULY 14

Honor God and He Will Honor You

Psalm 132 (NIV)

1. O Lord, remember David and all the <u>hardships he endured</u>.

2. He swore an oath to the Lord and made a vow to the mighty one of Jacob.

3. I will not enter my hour or go to my bed.

4. I will allow no sleep to my eyes, no slumber to my eyelids.

5. Till I find a place for the Lord, a dwelling place for the mighty one of Jacob. Amen

Our Iniquities

If thou, Lord shouldest mark iniquities, O Lord,
who shall stand?
Psalm 130:3

When I kept silence, my bones waxed old through my
roaring all the day long. I <u>acknowledge</u> my sin unto thee,
and mine iniquity have I unto the Lord; and thou forgavest
the iniquity of my sin.
Psalm 32:3, 5

I have gone astray like a lost sheep; seek thy servant for I do
not forget thy commandments.
Psalm 119:176

Our Iniquities

He that covereth his sins shall not prosper; but whoso confesseth a forsaken them shall have mercy.
Proverbs 28:13

Then said I woe is me! For I am undone; because I am a man of unclean lips: For mine eyes have seen the king, the Lord of host.
Isaiah 6:5

O God, thou knowest my foolishness: and my sins are not hid from thee.
Psalm 69:5

JULY 17

Integrity

For I know him, that he will command his children and his
household after him, and they shall keep the way of the
Lord, to do justice and judgment; that the Lord may bring up
Abraham that which he hath spoken of him.
Genesis 18:19

Integrity

My lips shall not speak wickedness, nor my tongue utter
deceit. God forbid that I should justify: Till I die I will not
remove mine <u>integrity</u> from me. My righteousness
I hold fast and will not let it go: My righteousness
I hold fast and will not let it go.
Job 27:46

The Lord rewarded me according to my righteousness:
According to the cleanness of my hands hath he
recompensed me.
Psalm 18:20

JULY 19

Worship

The Lord is my strength and song, and he is become my
salvation: he is my God. And I will prepare him a
habitation: my father's God, and I will exalt him.
Exodus 15:2

Give unto the Lord the glory due unto his name; worship the
Lord in the beauty of holiness.
Psalm 29:2

When I remember these things I pour out my soul in me: For
I had gone with the multitude, I went with them to the house
of God, with the voice of joy and praise, with a multitude
that kept holy day.
Psalm 42:4

JULY 20

Worship

O God, thou art my God; early will I seek thee: My soul thirsteth for thee, my flesh longeth for thee in a dry and thirsty land where no water is; to see thy power and thy glory, so as I have seen thee in the sanctuary.
Psalm 63:12

Thy way O God, is in the sanctuary who is so great a God as our God?
Psalm 77:13

JULY 21

In A Word

By: Max Lucado

Book: "Just Like Jesus"

Think for a moment about this question: What if God weren't here on earth? You think people can be cruel now, imagine us without the presence of God. You think we are brutal to each other now, imagine the world without the Holy Spirit.

You think there is loneliness and despair and guilt now, imagine life without the touch of Jesus.

No forgiveness, no hope, no acts of kindness, no words of love, no more food given in his name.

No more songs sung to praise him or song to his praise, no more deeds done in his honor.

If God took away his angels, his grace, his promise of eternity, and his servants what would the world be like?

In a word, hell.

JULY 22

The Word – Seed

All scripture is God–breathed and is useful for teaching, rebuking, correcting and training in righteousness, so that the man of God may be thoroughly equipped for every good work...the Holy Scriptures are able to make you wise for salvation through faith in Christ Jesus.

JULY 23

The Word – Seed

John 8:31-32 (TLB)

You are truly my disciples if you live as I tell you to, and you will know the truth, and the truth will (make) set you free.

Genesis 9:12-13

This is the sign of the covenant I am making between me and you and every living creature with you, a covenant for all generations to come:

JULY 24

The Word – Seed

Matthew 26:46 – Rise let us be going
"Let the past sleep, but let it sleep on the bosom of Christ, and go out into the irresistible future with Him."

"Arise and do the next thing."

If we are inspired of God, what is the next thing? To trust him absolutely and pray on the ground of his redemption never let the sense of failure corrupt your new action."

Quoted by: Oswald Chambers, "Upmost for His Highest"

In A Word

Grace and peace to you from him who is, and who was and who is to come, and from the seven spirits before his throne, and from Jesus Christ, who is the faithful witness, the firstborn from the dead, and the rule of the Kings of the earth. To him who loves us and freed us from our sins by his blood.

And has made us to be a kingdom and priests to serve his God and Father – to him be glory and power forever and ever! Amen.

JULY 26

In A Word

Your ears shall hear a word behind you, saying, "This is the way, walk in it," whenever you turn to the right hand or whenever you turn to the left.
Isaiah 30:21

JULY 27

Seed – Faith- Principle

Seed – The Word of GOD

My dear friend, keep this in mind, God's promise always turns on the light! So don't doubt what God says because you are experiencing some darkness. Stay focused! Most people miss their blessing simply because they allow their focus to be broken! Whenever I share these truths with you they must be spiritually discerned.

Peter was able to walk on water, as longs as he stayed focused. The enemy does not have to knock you out or bankrupt you to defeat you. He simply needs to "break your focus" and get you to look in another direction. Stay focus!

My dear friend, "I discern" you are receiving a witness in your spirit to go sow a seed of faith. Hosea 10:12 (AMP)

JULY 28

Seed – Faith – Principle

Sow for yourselves according to righteousness (uprightness and right standing with God) reap according to mercy and loving – kindness. Break up your uncultivated ground, for it is time to seek the Lord, to inquire for and of him and to inquire his favor, till he comes and teaches you righteousness and rains his righteousness gift of salvation upon you.

And (God) who provides seed from the sower and bread for eating will also provide and multiply your (resources for) sowing and increase the fruits of your righteousness (which manifests itself in active goodness, kindness, and charity).

2 Corinthians 9:10 (AMP)

JULY 29

Seed – Faith – Principle

Plant <u>goodness</u> (peace), harvest the fruit of <u>loyalty</u>, plow the new ground of <u>knowledge</u>.

Don't forget the <u>principle</u>. Never underestimate the power of (the) a seed.

He who received seed on good ground is he who hears the word and understands it, who indeed bear fruit and produces: some <u>a hundred fold</u>, <u>some sixty</u>, <u>some thirty</u>.
Matthew 13:23

JULY 30

Seed – Faith – Principle

The Seed, God's Word, is always good. It is the soil – the person's heart, personality, will and emotions – that must be prepared to receive Christ.

God's Word- some people are unreceptive, some are so-so and some are fertile and ready to burst forth with growth.

1.   Commit yourself to listening carefully.

2.   Resist all clutter (distraction).

3.   Evaluate your spiritual need right away.

Blessed are your eyes for they see, and your ears
for they hear.
Matthew 13:10-17

JULY 31

In A Word

"Incline your ear, and come unto me: hear and
your soul shall live."
Isaiah 55:3

John the Revelator

Hear what the Spirit is saying to the churches!!!
Revelation 1:4-6 (NIV)

AUGUST 1

Hear What The Spirit Is Saying (Isaiah 55:3)

Letters to the Churches:

The revelation of <u>John the Apostle</u> near the end of his life John had a vision concerning the seven churches <u>in Asia for the Christians</u>.

Revelation 1:1-3

The revelation of Jesus Christ, which God gave him to show his servants what must soon take place. He made it known by sending <u>his angel</u> to his servant <u>John</u> (Verse 2) who testifies to everything he saw – that is, the word of God and the testimony of Jesus Christ.

Blessed is the one who reads the words of this prophecy, and blessed are those who hear it and take it to heart what is written in it, because the time is near (verse 3).

He who has ears to hear, let him hear!
Matthew 13:9

AUGUST 2

The Plan of God

Every man's life is a plan of God.

By Horace Bughnell

AUGUST 3

The Plan of God

The Lord Almighty has sworn, surely, as I have planned so
it will be and as I have proposed, so it will stand.
Isaiah 14:24 (NIV)

AUGUST 4

The Plan of God

If you want to know what God wants you to do, ask him,
and he will gladly tell you, for he is always ready to
give a bountiful supply of wisdom to all who ask him;
he will not resent it.
James 1:5 (TLB)

AUGUST 5

The Plan – Vision

Make a plan to spend time with God, set aside quality time
for him. Put God first, he has to be first. For his
name's sake they went forth.
3 John 7 (NIV)

AUGUST 6

Faith

Read 2 Peter 1:5-8 (NIV)

Matthew 5:11-12 (TLB)

When you are reviled and persecuted and lied about because you are my followers – wonderful! Be happy about it. Be very glad! For a tremendous reward awaits you in heaven.

AUGUST 7

Strength

Isaiah 30:15
"In returning and rest shall be saved; in quietness and in confidence shall be your strength."

Habakkuk 3:19 (AMP)
The Lord God is my strength, my personal bravery, and my invincible army; He makes my feet like hinds feet and will make me to walk (not to stand still in terror, but to walk) and make (spiritual) progress upon my high places of trouble, suffering or responsibility!

AUGUST 8

Strength

The Lord is their strength, and he is the saving (power)
refuge of his anointed.
Psalm 28:8

Protection

Psalm 23:4 (TLB)

I will not be afraid, for you are close beside me, guarding, guiding all the way.

Death is not the enemy of life, but its friend, for it is the knowledge that our years are limited which makes them so precious. It is the truth that time is but lent to us which makes us, at our best look upon our years as a trust handed into our temporary keeping.

By Joshua Loth Liebman

AUGUST 10

Protection

Genesis 19:8
Look, I have two daughters who have never slept with a man. Let me bring them out to you, and you can do what you like with them. But don't do anything to these men, for they have come under the **protection** of my roof."

Exodus 22:1
[*Protection of Property*] "If a man steals an ox or a sheep and slaughters it or sells it, he must pay back five head of cattle for the ox and four sheep for the sheep.

AUGUST 11

Protection

Numbers 14:9
Only do not rebel against the LORD. And do not be afraid of the people of the land, because we will swallow them up. Their **protection** is gone, but the LORD is with us. Do not be afraid of them."

AUGUST 12

Protection

Numbers 32:17
But we are ready to arm ourselves and go ahead of the Israelites until we have brought them to their place. Meanwhile our women and children will live in fortified cities, for **protection** from the inhabitants of the land.

Joshua 20:3
So that anyone who kills a person accidentally and unintentionally may flee there and find **protection** from the avenger of blood.

AUGUST 13

Protection

Ezra 9:9

Though we are slaves, our God has not deserted us in our bondage. He has shown us kindness in the sight of the kings of Persia: He has granted us new life to rebuild the house of our God and repair its ruins, and he has given us a wall of **protection** in Judah and Jerusalem.

AUGUST 14

Protection

Psalm 5:11
But let all who take refuge in you be glad; let them ever sing for joy. Spread your **protection** over them, that those who love your name may rejoice in you.

Isaiah 30:2
Who go down to Egypt without consulting me; who look for help to Pharaoh's **protection**, to Egypt's shade for refuge.

 AUGUST 15

Protection

Isaiah 30:3
But Pharaoh's **protection** will be to your shame, Egypt's shade will bring you disgrace.

Micah 1:11
Pass on in nakedness and shame, you who live in Shaphir. [Shaphir means pleasant.] Those who live in Zaanan [Zaanan sounds like the Hebrew for come out.] will not come out. Beth Ezel is in mourning; its **protection** is taken from you.

AUGUST 16

The Lord Our Protector

If you make the Most High your dwelling then no harm will befall you, no disaster will near your tent.

He who watches over you will not slumber.

The Lord is your shade at your right hand; the sun will not harm you by day, nor the moon by night. The Lord will keep you from all harm.
Psalm 91:9-10, 121:3, 3, 5-7

AUGUST 17

The Lord Our Protector

Those who go to God Most High for safety will be protected by the Almighty.
Psalm 91:1

AUGUST 18

Heaven's On Your Side

By Max Lucado
Book: When Christ Comes

Jesus is praying for us. Jesus has spoken and Satan has listened, the devil may land a punch or two. He may even win a few rounds but he never wins the fight. Why? Because Jesus takes up for you..."He is able always to save those who come to God through him because he always lives, asking God to help them" **Hebrews 7:25.**

Jesus at this very moment is protecting you. Evil must pass through Christ before it can touch you. And God will "never let you be pushed past the limit; he'll always be there to help you come through it."
(1 Corinthians 10:13 MSG).

AUGUST 19

Heaven's On Your Side

The one who died for us: Is in the presence of God at this very moment sticking for us.
Romans 8:34 (MSG)

AUGUST 20

Heaven's On Your Side

To whom will you compare me? Or who is my equal? Say the Holy One. Lift your eyes and look to the heavens: Who created all these? He who brings out the starry hosts one by one, and calls them each by name. Because of his great power and mighty strength, no one of them is missing.
Isaiah 40:25-26 (NIV)

AUGUST 21

Heaven's On Your Side

Do you know? Have you not heard? The Lord is the everlasting God, the creator of the ends of the earth. He will not grow tired or weary, and his understanding no one can fathom. He gives strength to the weary and increase the power to the wealth.

Isaiah 40:28-29 (NIV)

AUGUST 22

Be Still and Know that (He) is God

When we see the lilies spinning in distress, taking thought to manufacture loveliness. When we see the birds all building barns for store. "Twill be time for us to worry, not before.

Be still, my anxious heart **(Psalm 46:10)**.

Be still, and know that I am God.

AUGUST 23

His Hand

Whoever falls from God's hand is caught into his left.
(Quoted by Edwin Markham)

I will not forget you!
(Isaiah 49:15)

AUGUST 24

His Hand

Have set the Lord continually before me; because he is at my right hand, I shall not be moved. Therefore my heart is glad and my glory (my inner self rejoices; my body too shall rest and confidently dwell in safety).
Psalm 16:89 (AMP)

AUGUST 25

His Hand

I want men everywhere to lift up holy hands in prayer,
without anger or disputing.
1 Timothy 2:8

AUGUST 26

His Hand

Then King David went in and sat before the Lord, and said,
"Who am I, O Sovereign Lord, and what is my family, that
you have brought me this far?"
2 Samuel 7:18

AUGUST 27

His Hand

John the Baptist said, "Repent for the kingdom of heaven is at hand!"
(Matthew 3:2)

AUGUST 28

The Kingdom of God

For the kingdom is the Lord's: and he is the governor
among the nations
(Psalms 22:28)

AUGUST 29

Haters Elevate You

Encourage those who are afraid. Tell them, "Be strong fear
not, for your God is coming to destroy your enemies.
He is coming to save you."
Isaiah 35:4 (TLB)

AUGUST 30

Prayer

Changes

Things

Psalm 145:18 (NIV)

The Lord is near to all who call on him, to all who call on
him (in truth).

AUGUST 31

Peace

Rest

Among

You

SEPTEMBER 1

Prayer Changes Things

Trouble and perplexity drive us to prayer and prayer, driveth away trouble and perplexity.
By Philip Melanchton

SEPTEMBER 2

Prayer

I love the Lord because he hears my prayers and
answer them.
Psalm 116:1 (TLB)

SEPTEMBER 3

The Light of God's Presence

If we are living in the light of God's presence, just as Christ does, then we have wonderful fellowship and joy with each other, and the Blood of Jesus, his Son cleanses us from every sin. Amen.
1 John 1:7 (TLB)

(Labor Day)

SEPTEMBER 4

MARY

Luke 10:39, 42
"Mary...sat at Jesus feet and heard his Word...Mary hath
chosen that good part which shall not be taken
away from her."

Messiah
Almighty
Reedemer
Yaweh – Lord – God

SEPTEMBER 5

Cleanse Me, Master

Pray:
Master; expose the true devotion of my heart. Cleanse me, make me a temple fit for your presence. Amen!

SEPTEMBER 6

Cleanse Me

Psalm 51:2 (NIV)
Wash away all my iniquity and **cleanse me** from my sin.

SEPTEMBER 7

Cleanse Me

Psalm 51:7 (NIV)
Cleanse me with hyssop, and I will be clean; wash **me**, and I will be whiter than snow.

SEPTEMBER 8

Cleanse Me

Jeremiah 33:8 (NIV)
I will **cleanse** them from all the sin thy have committed against **me** and will forgive all their sins of rebellion against **me**.

SEPTEMBER 9

Joy

Job 8:21 (NIV)
He will yet fill your mouth with laughter and your lips with shouts of **joy**.

SEPTEMBER 10

Joy

Psalm 89:15

Blessed is the people that know the **joy**ful sound: they shall walk, O **LORD**, in the light of thy countenance.

SEPTEMBER 11

Joyful Noise

Psalm 95:1
O come, let us sing unto the **LORD**: let us make a **joy**ful noise to the rock of our salvation.

SEPTEMBER 12

Joyful Noise

Psalm 98:4

Make a **joy**ful noise unto the **LORD,** all the earth: make a loud noise, and rejoice, and sing praise.

SEPTEMBER 13

Strength

2 Samuel 22:33
God is my **strength** and power: and he maketh
my way perfect.

(Rosh Hashana)

SEPTEMBER 14

Strength

2 Samuel 22:40

For thou hast girded me with **strength** to battle: them that rose up against me hast thou subdued under me.

SEPTEMBER 15

Victory

1 Corinthians 15:55
O death, where is thy sting? O grave, where is thy **victory**?

SEPTEMBER 16

Victory

1 Corinthians 15:57
But thanks be to God, which giveth us the **victory** through our Lord Jesus Christ.

SEPTEMBER 17

Victory

1 John 5:4

For whatsoever is born of God overcometh the world: and this is the **victory** that overcometh the world, even our faith.

SEPTEMBER 18

Grace

2 Corinthians 12:9

And he said unto me, My **grace is sufficient** for thee: for my strength **is** made perfect in weakness. Most gladly therefore will I rather glory in my infirmities, that the power of Christ may rest upon me.

SEPTEMBER 19

Grace

Psalm 45:2
Thou art fairer than the children of men: **grace** is poured into thy lips: therefore God hath blessed thee for ever.

SEPTEMBER 20

Grace

Psalm 84:11
For the LORD God is a sun and shield: the LORD will give
grace and glory: no good thing will he withhold
from them that walk uprightly.

SEPTEMBER 21

Eternal Life

John 3:15
That whosoever believeth in him should not perish, but have **eternal life**.

John 3:16
For God so loved the world, that he gave his only begotten Son, that whosoever believeth in him should not perish, but have everlasting life.

SEPTEMBER 22

Eternal Life

Matthew 19:16
And, behold, one came and said unto him, Good Master, what good thing shall I do, that I may have **eternal life**?

Mark 10:30
But he shall receive an hundredfold now in this time, houses, and brethren, and sisters, and mothers, and children, and lands, with persecutions; and in the world to come
eternal life.
(Yom Kippur)

SEPTEMBER 23

Eternal Life

Matthew 25:46
And these shall go away into everlasting punishment: but the righteous into **life eternal**.
(Autumn Begins)

SEPTEMBER 24

Eternal Life

Mark 10:17

And when he was gone forth into the way, there came one running, and kneeled to him, and asked him, Good Master, what shall I do that I may inherit **eternal life**?

SEPTEMBER 25

Eternal Life

Luke 10:25
And, behold, a certain lawyer stood up, and tempted him, saying, Master, what shall I do to inherit **eternal life**?

Luke 18:18
And a certain ruler asked him, saying, Good Master, what shall I do to inherit **eternal life**?

SEPTEMBER 26

The Lord's Name is Excellent

Psalm 8:1
O LORD, our Lord, how **excellent is thy name** in all the earth! who hast set **thy** glory above the heavens.

Psalm 8:9
O LORD our Lord, how **excellent is thy name** in all the earth!

SEPTEMBER 27

Worship

GOD WANTS YOUR WORSHIP!
SO WORSHIP HIM RIGHT NOW!
HE IS THE REASON FOR YOUR WORSHIP.
WORSHIP, WORSHIP,
WORSHIP HIM TODAY!

SEPTEMBER 28

Worship

Joshua 5:14
And he said, Nay; but as captain of the host of the LORD am I now come. And Joshua fell on his face to the earth, and did **worship**, and said unto him, What saith my Lord unto his servant?

Judges 7:15
And it was so, when Gideon heard the telling of the dream, and the interpretation thereof, that he **worship**ped, and returned into the host of Israel, and said, Arise; for the LORD hath delivered into your hand the host of Midian.

SEPTEMBER 29

Worship

1 Samuel 1:3
And this man went up out of his city yearly to worship and to sacrifice unto the LORD of hosts in Shiloh. And the two sons of Eli, Hophni and Phinehas, the priests of the LORD, were there.

1 Samuel 1:19
And they rose up in the morning early, and worshipped before the LORD, and returned, and came to their house to Ramah: and Elkanah knew Hannah his wife; and the LORD remembered her.

SEPTEMBER 30

Worship

1 Samuel 1:3
And this man went up out of his city yearly to worship and to sacrifice unto the LORD of hosts in Shiloh. And the two sons of Eli, Hophni and Phinehas, the priests of the LORD, were there.

1 Samuel 1:19
And they rose up in the morning early, and worshipped before the LORD, and returned, and came to their house to Ramah: and Elkanah knew Hannah his wife; and the LORD remembered her.

OCTOBER 1

Patience

James 5:7, 8 (NIV)

Be patient, then, brothers, until the LORD's coming. See how the farmer waits for the land to yield its valuable crop and how patient he is for the autumn and spring rains.

You too, be patient and stand firm, because the LORD's coming is near.

1 Peter 2:20 (NIV)

But how is it to your credit if you receive a beating for doing wrong and endure it? But if you suffer for doing good and you endure it, this is commendable before God.

OCTOBER 2

Patience

Galatians 6:9 (NIV)
Let us not become weary in doing good, for at the proper time we will reap a harvest if we do not give up.

Hebrews 10:23 (NIV)
Let us hold unswervingly to the hope we profess, for he who promised is faithful.

OCTOBER 3

Patience

Matthew 24:13 (NIV)
But he who stands firm to the end will be saved.

Hebrews 6:12 (NIV)
We do not want you to become lazy, but to imitate those who through faith and patience inherit what has been promised.

(Last Day of Sukkot)

OCTOBER 4

Patience Is of the Essence

Be patient with me!
The Lord is not finished with me yet!

He knows when I am weak,
He knows when I am strong,
He knows when I can't go on.

Be patient with me!
The Lord is not finished with me yet!

Why do we continue to rush?
When the Lord is already handling all of your stuff!
So why not live in patience?
Since the LORD IS PATIENCE!

Be patient with me!
The Lord is not finished with me yet!

Patience is of the essence
So that we can enter into God's presence
To get our daily lessons
And the many blessings.

So be patient with me!
The Lord is not finished with me yet!

OCTOBER 5

Praise

2 Samuel 22:4
I will call on the LORD, who is worthy to be **praise**d: so shall I be saved from mine enemies.

2 Samuel 22:50
Therefore I will give thanks unto thee, O LORD, among the heathen, and I will sing **praise**s unto thy name.

OCTOBER 6

Praise

1 Chronicles 16:25
For great is the LORD, and greatly to be **praise**d: he also is to be feared above all gods.

1 Chronicles 16:35
And say ye, Save us, O God of our salvation, and gather us together, and deliver us from the heathen, that we may give thanks to thy holy name, and glory in thy **praise**.

1 Chronicles 16:36
Blessed be the LORD God of Israel for ever and ever. And all the people said, Amen, and **praise**d the LORD.

OCTOBER 7

Praise

1 Chronicles 23:5
Moreover four thousand were porters; and four thousand **praise**d the LORD with the instruments which I made, said David, to **praise** therewith.

1 Chronicles 23:30
And to stand every morning to thank and **praise** the LORD, and likewise at even:

OCTOBER 8

The Glory of the Lord

Exodus 40:34
Then a cloud covered the tent of the congregation, and the **glory** of the LORD filled the tabernacle.

Exodus 40:35
And Moses was not able to enter into the tent of the congregation, because the cloud abode thereon, and the **glory** of the LORD filled the tabernacle.

(Columbus Day)

OCTOBER 9

The Glory of the Lord

Leviticus 9:6
And Moses said, This is the thing which the LORD commanded that ye should do: and the **glory** of the LORD shall appear unto you.

Leviticus 9:23
And Moses and Aaron went into the tabernacle of the congregation, and came out, and blessed the people: and the **glory** of the LORD appeared unto all the people.

OCTOBER 10

The Glory of the Lord

Numbers 14:10
But all the congregation bade stone them with stones. And the **glory** of the LORD appeared in the tabernacle of the congregation before all the children of Israel.

Numbers 14:21
But as truly as I live, all the earth shall be filled with the **glory** of the LORD.

OCTOBER 11

Faith

Psalm 101:6

Mine eyes shall be upon the **faith**ful of the land, that they may dwell with me: he that walketh in a perfect way, he shall serve me.

Psalm 119:75

I know, O LORD, that thy judgments are right, and that thou in **faith**fulness hast afflicted me.

OCTOBER 12

Faith

Proverbs 13:17
A wicked messenger falleth into mischief: but a **faith**ful
ambassador is health.

Proverbs 14:5
A **faith**ful witness will not lie: but a false witness
will utter lies.

OCTOBER 13

Faith

Psalm 143:1

Hear my prayer, O LORD, give ear to my supplications: in thy **faith**fulness answer me, and in thy righteousness.

Proverbs 11:13

A talebearer revealeth secrets: but he that is of a **faith**ful spirit concealeth the matter.

OCTOBER 14

Faith

Psalm 119:86
All thy commandments are **faith**ful: they persecute me
wrongfully; help thou me.

Psalm 119:90
Thy **faith**fulness is unto all generations: thou hast
established the earth, and it abideth.

Psalm 119:138
Thy testimonies that thou hast commanded are righteous and
very **faith**ful.

OCTOBER 15

Faith

Freedom

Almighty

Integrity

Thankful

Healer

OCTOBER 16

Hope

Psalm 16:9
Therefore my heart is glad, and my glory rejoiceth: my flesh also shall rest in **hope**.

Psalm 22:9
But thou art he that took me out of the womb: thou didst make me **hope** when I was upon my mother's breasts.

OCTOBER 17

Hope

Psalm 31:24
Be of good courage, and he shall strengthen your heart, all
ye that **hope** in the LORD.

Psalm 33:18
Behold, the eye of the LORD is upon them that fear him,
upon them that **hope** in his mercy;

OCTOBER 18

Hope

Psalm 33:22
Let thy mercy, O LORD, be upon us, according as we
hope in thee.

OCTOBER 19

Hope

Psalm 38:15

For in thee, O LORD, do I **hope**: thou wilt hear,
O Lord my God.

OCTOBER 20

Hope

In God There Is Hope!

Hope is what we need to go on each day!

OCTOBER 21

Happiness

Job 5:17
Behold, **happy** is the man whom God correcteth: therefore despise not thou the chastening of the Almighty:

Psalm 127:5
Happy is the man that hath his quiver full of them: they shall not be ashamed, but they shall speak with the enemies in the gate.

Psalm 128:2
For thou shalt eat the labour of thine hands: **happy** shalt thou be, and it shall be well with thee.

OCTOBER 22

Happiness

Psalm 144:15
Happy is that people, that is in such a case: yea, **happy** is that people, whose God is the LORD.

Psalm 146:5
Happy is he that hath the God of Jacob for his help, whose hope is in the LORD his God:

OCTOBER 23

Pray

Until

Something

Happens

OCTOBER 24

PUSH

Pray **U**ntil **S**omething **H**appens

(Used by the permission of God promises for you, published by Daily Blessing, Inc.; Scripture quotes used by permission of Tyndal House Publishing).

Prince of
Righteousness
And
Your
Eternal
Rewarder

By William Carey
Prayer – secret, fervent.
Believing prayer – lies at the root of all personal godliness.

OCTOBER 25

Prayer Changes Things

"In everything by prayer and supplication let your requests be made known unto God."

"If we ask anything according to His will, he heareth us: And it we know that he hear us, whatsoever we ask, we know that we have the petitions that we desired of him."

John 5:14-15

OCTOBER 26

Prayer Makes A Difference

We all know that God does not listen to sinners but he listen
to anyone who worships and obey him.
John 9:31

OCTOBER 27

Prayer

Devote yourselves to prayer
(Colossians 4:2 NRSV)

OCTOBER 28

Prayer

John Vianney
The more we pray, the more we wish to pray. Amen!

OCTOBER 29

Prayer

Philippians 4:6—Phillips
Don't worry over anything, whenever you pray tell God
every detail of your needs in thankful prayer.

OCTOBER 30

Prayer

John 17:6, 9, 10, 24

You gave them to me and they have obeyed your word…I pray for them. I am not praying for the world, but for those you have given me, for they are yours and glory has come to me through me…Father I want those you gave have given me to be with me where I am and too see my glory.

"In everything by prayer and supplication let your request be made known unto God."

OCTOBER 31

Peace

Philippians 4:7 – The Lord our Peace

Judges 65:24 – Gideon built an altar and named it Jehovah Shalom, the Lord Our Peace

Peace
Rest
Among
You

(Halloween)

NOVEMBER 1

Trust

2 Corinthians 2:15 – I will very gladly spend and be spent for you.

NOVEMBER 2

Trust

Romans 8:14 - Be in all things led by the Spirit of God.

NOVEMBER 3

Trust

Proverbs 8:34 – Blessed is the man that heareth me watching daily at my gates, waiting at the post of my doors.

Jeremiah 45:5 - Thy life will I give for a prey in all places whether thou goest.

NOVEMBER 4

Prayer

2 Chronicles 7:12-18

(Charles Stanley)

Solomon had just completed the construction of the temple. Sacrifices were made to God along with a commitment to follow the Lord all the days of his life.

God was pleased, and in 2 Chronicles, he acknowledges Solomon's devotion: "My eyes shall open and my ears attentive to prayer offered in this place."

As Solomon stepped back and viewed the glory of the temple of God, he has struck with awesome reality of God's presence all about him.

The Shekinah glory of God literally filled the place. When you pray allow God to expose the true devotion of your heart. Ask him to cleanse you and make you a temple for his presence.

(Daylight Savings Time Ends)

NOVEMBER 5

Prayer

1 Kings 8:52-60 (NIV)

Solomon's prayer forgiveness of sin for his people & also being committed to the Lord's ways and commands at all times.

Solomon had got (insight) prophetic insight for his people so he would pray for the nations as well as for his people of Israel. And then future captivities and would ask God to be merciful to them as they cried out to him (2 Kings 17:25). And forgive and return them to their homeland (Reference: Ezra 1:2, Nehemiah 1:2)

NOVEMBER 6

Prayer

Deuteronomy 28-61

Obey or the Lord will bring all kinds of sickness and diseases not recorded in this Book of the Law.

Read Deuteronomy 7:15-19

NOVEMBER 7

Prayer Keys to the Kingdom

Obedience is better than sacrifice!

1 Corinthians 15:55-57 (AMP)

O death, where is your victory? O death where is your sting of death, and sin exercises its power (upon the soul) through (the abuse of) the Law. But thanks be to God, who gives us victory (making us conquerors) through our Lord Jesus Christ.

NOVEMBER 8

Our Sin

Psalm 103:12 (TLB)

He has removed our sins as far away from us as the east is from the west.

NOVEMBER 9

Our Sin

Luke 15:10 (AMP)

Even so, I tell you, there is very joy among and is the presence of the angels of God over one (especially) wicked person who repents (changes) his mind for the better, heartily amending his ways, with abhorrence of his past sins.

NOVEMBER 10

Our Sin

Romans 6:23 (NASB)
For the wages of sin is death, but the free gift of God is
eternal life in Christ
Jesus our Lord.

NOVEMBER 11

Our Sin

Romans 6:23

All have sinned and fall short of the glory of God.
(Quote by Charles Stanley on Holy Ground)

Repentance-a sincere devotion to Christ, separate a person from natural ways of the world. Many people need God's forgiveness, but they resist any involvement with him that disrupts their present lifestyle. True repentance is a humble, quiet, life-changing experience between you and God. It involves a renewing of your mind and offers a new perspective on life-one of hope and lasting joy. Through repentance, we turn away from sin completely. W. E. Vines defines this as "the adjustment of moral and spiritual vision and thinking to that of the mind of God, which is designed to have transforming effect upon the life." Romans 12:2 (NASB) – Do not be conformed to this world, but be transformed by the renewing of your mind.

(Veteran's Day)

NOVEMBER 12

Our Sin

Master, I answer your call today, adjust my moral and spiritual vision, align my thinking with yours. Renew my mind, transform my life.

(Veteran's Day Observed)

NOVEMBER 13

Our Sin

Genesis 5:3, Psalm 51:5, Romans 7:15, 1 Corinthians 15:57

Adam had a son in his own likeness – surely I was sinful at birth, sinful from the time my mother conceived me. I do not understand what I do for what I want to do I do not do, but what I hat I do, but thanks be to God! He gives us the victory through our Lord Jesus Christ.

NOVEMBER 14

The Power of Wealth and Eternal Riches

"Continually go back to the foundation of your affections and recollect where the source of power is." (By Oswald Chambers-Upmost for His Highest)

"And when he heard this, he was sorrowful:
For he was very rich."
(Luke 18:23)

NOVEMBER 15

Christ In You

How does God himself, whose immensity cannot be measured, reside in such frail bodies as our? How does the transcendent Christ live in finite human temples?

We may not comprehend the vastness of this principle, yet the method by which God imparts his presence is plain and clear in scriptures: Christ lives in us through His indwelling Holy Spirit. The Holy Spirit supernaturally brings the reality of Christ into our earthly frames. As the third person of the Trinity, the Holy Spirit is just as much deity as the Father and the Son. He imparts the life of Christ to us through His residence in our lives. The Holy Spirit reveals and shares with us all that Christ is. By making His home in us, He assures us of the presence and power of the risen Christ. Because the Holy Spirit possesses all the attributes of deity and because He inhabits our mortal bodies, He is infinitely adequate to meet any of our needs. He is not a God far off but a God who is near.

The resurrected Christ is your sure and steadfast hope for all of life, a hope that is every believer's to claim because of the indwelling ministry of the Holy Spirit.

By Charles Stanley

NOVEMBER 16

Christ In You

John 16:4

He will glorify me, for he will take of what is mine and declare it to you.

Come Holy Spirit, and do your work. Reveal all that Christ is and wants to be to me. Give me assurance of His presence and power. Let the same Spirit who raised Christ from the dead work abundantly in me.

NOVEMBER 17

Fear Not

Isaiah 41:10 (TLB)
Fear not, I am with you. Do not be dismayed. I am your God. I will strengthen you; I will help you; I will uphold you with my victorious right hand.

Exodus 23:20
"I'm sending an angel ahead of you to guard you along the way and bring you to the place I have prepared."

NOVEMBER 18

Fear Not

2 Corinthians 7:1 (TLB)
"Having such promises as these, dear friends, let us turn away from everything wrong...giving ourselves to him alone."

Psalm 91:4
He shall cover thee with his feathers and under his wings shalt thou trust take one hour. Write the Vision.

NOVEMBER 19

Do Not Fear – Do Not Be Afraid
For the Lord Thy God Is With You (Us)

Proverbs 3:24
When you lie down you will not be afraid: When you lie
down, your sleep will be sweet.

Psalm 4:8
I will lie down and sleep in peace, for you alone, O Lord
make me dwell in safety.

Psalm 127:2
He grants sleep (peace) to those he loves.

NOVEMBER 20

<u>You Must Trust</u>

You must trust me wholly; this lesson has to be learned. You shall be helped; you shall be led, guided continually. The children of Israel would long before have entered the Promised Land – only their doubts and fears continually drove them back into the wilderness. Remember always, doubts delay. Are you trusting all to me or not? I have told you how to live and you must do it. My children, I love you. Trust my tender love. It will never fail you, but you must learn not to fail it. Oh! could you see, you would understand. You have much to learn in turning out fear and being at peace. All your doubts arrest my work. You must not doubt. I died to save you from sin and doubt and worry.

You must believe in me absolutely.

(Published by Barbour and Company, Inc.)

NOVEMBER 21

Trust

Jeremiah 17:7
The person who trusts the Lord will be blessed.

Job 23:12 (NAS)
I have treasured the words of His mouth more than my necessary food.

2 Corinthians 1:9 (TM)
We were forced to Trust God Totally."

NOVEMBER 22

Trust in the Lord

Romans 12:13
Share with God's people who are in need.

Matthew 25:35-36
"I was hungry and you have me something to eat, I was thirsty and you have me something to drink. I was a stranger and you invited me in, I needed clothes and you clothed me." (Jesus speaking)

(Thanksgiving Day)

NOVEMBER 23

Trust in the Lord

Hebrews 13:16

Do not forget to do good and to share with others, with such sacrifices God is pleased.

John 6:35 (AMP)

Jesus replied, I am the bread of life. He who comes to me will never be hungry, and he who believes in and cleaves to and trusts in and relies on me will never thirst anymore (at any time).

NOVEMBER 24

A Broken Heart

Perhaps the <u>wound </u>is old. A parent <u>abused</u> you. A teacher <u>slighted</u> you. A mate <u>betrayed</u> you, and you are <u>angry</u>.

Or perhaps the wound is fresh. The friend who owes you money just drove by in a new car. The boss who hired you with promises of promotions has forgotten how to pronounce your name. And you are <u>hurt</u>. Part of you is <u>broken</u>, and the other part is <u>bitter</u>. Part of you want to <u>cry</u> and part of you want to <u>fight</u>. There is a fire burning in your heart. It's the fire of anger. And you are left with a decision. Do I put the fire out or heat it up? Do I get over it or get even? Do I release it or resent it. Do I let my hurts heal or do I let hurt turn into hate? Unfaithfulness is wrong. Revenge is bad. But the worst part of all is that, without forgiveness, bitterness is all that is left.

Amen

NOVEMBER 25

A Broken Heart

Psalm 147:3 (NIV) – He heals the brokenhearted and binds up their wounds.

Happiness is inward and not outward; and so it does not depend on what we have, but on what we are. (Quote by Henry van Dyke, "Antique Rose Teaport, Zondervan Bible Publishers)

Psalm 61:2 (TLB) – When my heart is faint and overwhelmed, lead me to the mighty towering Rock of safety.

NOVEMBER 26

The New Heart

Ezekiel 36:26 (TLB)

I will give you a new heart – I will give you new and right desires – and put a new spirit within you. I will take out your stony hearts of sin and give you new hearts of love.

1 Samuel 16:7

"The Lord seeth not as man seeth; for man looked on the outward appearance but the Lord looketh on the heart."

NOVEMBER 27

Strength

Zechariah 4:6 (TLB)

Not by might nor by power, but by my Spirit, says the Lord Almighty – you will succeed because of my Spirit, though you are few and weak.

Nahum 1:7

The Lord is good a strength and stronghold in the day of trouble; He knows (recognizes, has knowledge of, and understands) those who take refuge and trust in him.

NOVEMBER 28

Strength

Hebrews 13:5 (NIV)
God has said "Never will I leave you; never will I forsake you."

Isaiah 30:15
"In returning and rest shall ye be saved; in quietness and in confidence shall be your strength."

NOVEMBER 29

Comfort in the Time of Need

2 Corinthians 1:3, 4 (NIV)

The God of all comforts us in all our troubles, so that we can comfort those in any trouble with the comfort we ourselves have received from God.

In whatever God does in the course of our lives, He gives us through the experience, some power to help others. (Elisabeth Elliot)

A heart stitched with prayer is more precious to God than a tapestry of gold.

NOVEMBER 30

God Calling: Nothing Is Too Small

Nothing is small to God. In his sight a sparrow is of greater value than a palace, one kindly word or more importance than a statesman's speech. It is the life in all that has value and the quality of life that determines the value. I came to give eternal life.

Matthew 10:29-31

"Are not two sparrows sold for a penny? Yet not one of them will fall to the ground apart from the will of your Father – And even the very hairs of your head are all numbered. So don't be afraid; you are worth more than many sparrows."

DECEMBER 1

Climate for Healing

Matthew 15:27-28

27 And he said, "Yes, Lord, yet even the little dogs eat the crumbs which fall from their masters' table."

28 Then Jesus answered and said to her, "O woman, great [is] your faith! Let it be to you as you desire." And her daughter was healed from that very hour.

DECEMBER 2

Climate for Healing

Mark 5:29-31

29 Immediately the fountain of blood was dried up, and she felt in [her] body that she was healed of the affliction.

30 And Jesus, immediately knowing in Himself that power had gone out of Him, turned around in the crowd and said, "who touched My clothes?"

31 But His disciples said to Him, "You see the multitude thronging You, and You say, 'Who touched Me?'"

DECEMBER 3

Climate for Healing

Mark 5:32-34

32 And He looked around to see her who had done this thing.

33 But the woman, fearing and trembling, knowing what had happened to her, came and fell down before Him and told Him the whole truth.

34 And He said to her, "Daughter, your faith has made you well. Go in peace, and be healed of your affliction."

DECEMBER 4

Climate for Healing

Matthew 9:27-28

27 When Jesus departed from there, two blind men followed Him, crying out and saying, "Son of David, have mercy on us!"

28 And when He had come into the house, the blind men came to Him, and Jesus said to them, "Do you believe that I am able to do this?" They said to him, Yes, Lord."

DECEMBER 5

Climate for Healing

Matthew 9:29-30

29 Then He touched their eyes, saying, "According to your faith let it be to you."

30 And their eyes were opened. And Jesus sternly warned them, saying, "see [that] no one knows [it."]]

(First Day of Chanukah)

DECEMBER 6

Climate for Healing

Matthew 15:21-25

21 Then Jesus went out from there and departed to the region of Tyre and Sidon.

22 And behold, a woman of Canaan came from that region and cried out to Him, saying, "Have mercy on me, O Lord, Son of David! My daughter is severely demon-possessed."

23 But he answered her not a word. And His disciples came and urged Him, saying, "Send her away, for she cries out after us."

24 But He answered and said, "I was not sent except to the lost sheep of the house of Israel."

25 Then she came and worshipped Him, saying, "Lord, help me!"

Mark 5:27-28

27 When she heard about Jesus, she came behind [Him] in the crowd and touched His garment.

28 For she said, "If only I may touch His clothes, I shall be made well."

DECEMBER 7

Climate for Healing

Acts 1:14

14 These all continued with one accord in prayer and supplication, with the women and Mary the mother of Jesus, and with His brothers.

Acts 2:1

1 When the Day of Pentecost had fully come, they were all with one accord in one place.

Acts 2:46

46 So continuing daily with one accord in the temple, and breaking bread from house to house, they ate their food with gladness and simplicity of heart,

Acts 4:24

24 So when they heard that, they raised their voice to God with one accord and said: "Lord You [are] God, who made heaven and earth and the sea, and all that is in them,

Acts 5:12

12 And through the hands of the apostles many signs and wonders were done among the people. And they were all with one accord in Solomon's Porch.

All scriptures taken from the New King James Version of the Bible

DECEMBER 8

Fear/False
Evident
Appearing/Acting
Real

Proverbs 3:25 (NIV)

Have no fear of sudden disaster or of the ruin that overtakes the wicked, for the Lord will be your confidence and will keep your foot from being snared.

DECEMBER 9

Healing

1. For what do we need to be healed? From what do we need to be healed?

1. Sickness – Luke 8:42, Mark 1:40
2. A broken heart – Isaiah 61:1
3. Sorrow – Psalm 30:11
4. Betrayed – Psalm 55:20
5. To forgive – Psalm 103:3-4, forgive our sin (Romans 6:23)

DECEMBER 10

Healing

2. How does God Heal?

1.Through physician and medicine – 2 Kings 20:7, Psalm 119:93, Mark 3:5;

1.   Through agony – Psalm 6:2
2.   Through prayer – James 5:13-16
3.   Through discipline – Isaiah 38:16
4.   Through time – Genesis 27:41, Genesis 33:4
5.   Through the faith of friend – Mark 2:1-5
6.   Through miracles – Luke 5:12-13

DECEMBER 11

Healing

By death Christ brought us life. Through woundedness he brought us healing. By accepting our punishment, he set us free **(Isaiah 53:5)**.

DECEMBER 12

Healing

3. Why doesn't God always heal people?

2 Corinthians 12:8-9 - My power works best in weakness. God's power is magnified through our weaknesses and infirmities, if we allow him to work within us.

(Last Day of Chanukah)

DECEMBER 13

Healing

4. How do I deal with it when I'm not healed?

2 Corinthians 12:10 – We can look forward to having God's power work through us in a special way. When God works through the weak it is obvious that what occurred had to happened because of him thus showing the world his love and power.

DECEMBER 14

Healing

Malachi 4:2 – But for you who fear my name the Sun of Righteousness will rise with healing in his wings. And you will go free leaping with joy like calves let out to pasture.

Sun and Air are my great healing forces **(Malachi 4:2)**

DECEMBER 15

Healing

Isaiah 61:1&2
The Spirit of the Lord God is upon me because the Lord hath anointed me to preach good (news) tidings unto the poor (meek) he hath sent me to bind up the brokenhearted, to proclaim liberty (freedom) to the captives and the opening (release) of the prison or (prisoner) from darkness to proclaim the acceptable year of the Lord, and the day of vengeance of our God; to comfort all that mourn. Amen

Psalm 11:3
If the foundation be destroyed what can the righteous do?

DECEMBER 16

Healing

When the Lord chose you to be pulled out of darkness and walk in the light this is what happened. You might be overwhelmed; you might have been crushed.

But God said in his Word,
Isaiah 54:17: No weapon that is formed against thee shall prosper, and every tongue that shall rise against thee in judgment thou shall condemn. This is the heritage of the servants of the Lord and their righteous is of me saith the Lord.

AMEN!!

DECEMBER 17

LIVE

1 Peter 3:9 (AMP)
Never return evil for evil or insult for insult (scolding, tongue –lashing, berating), but on the contrary blessing (praying for their welfare, happiness, and protection, and truly pitying and loving them). For to know that to this you have been called, that you may yourselves inherit a blessing (from God – that you may obtain a blessing as heirs, bringing welfare and happiness and protection).

Psalm 25: 1 & 2 (AMP)
Unto you, O Lord, do I bring my life. O my God, I trust, lean on, rely on, and am confident in you. Let me not be put to shame or (my hope in you) be disappointed; let not my enemies triumph over me.

DECEMBER 18

Live

Matthew 18:11
For the Son of man came to save (from the penalty of eternal death) pay that which was lost (Zondervan Publishing House).

Ephesians 2:1
As for you, you were dead in your transgressions and sins, in which you used to live when you followed the ways of this world and the ruler of the kingdom of the air, the spirit who is now at work in those who are disobedient. All of us also lived among them at one time, gratifying the cravings of our sinful nature, and following its desires and thoughts. Like the rest, we were by nature objects of wrath.

DECEMBER 19

Live

Romans 1:18

[18]The wrath of God is being revealed from heaven against all the godlessness and wickedness of men who suppress the truth by their wickedness, [19]since what may be known about God is plain to them. [20]For since the creation of the world God's invisible qualities – his eternal powers and divine nature –have been clearly seen, being understood from what has been made, so that men are without excuse. [21]For although they knew God, they neither glorified him as God nor gave thanks to him but their thinking became futile and their foolish hearts were darkened.

Hosea 12:6 (TLB)

Live by the principles of love and justice, and always be expecting much from him, your God.

DECEMBER 20

Live

Psalm 34:11 (NIV)
Come my children, listen to me. I will teach you the fear of the Lord. Whoever of you love life and desires to see many good days keep your lips from speaking lies, turn from evil and do good; seek peace and pursue it.

Titus 1:15 (TLB)
A person who is pure of heart sees goodness and purity in everything; but a person whose heart is evil and untrusting finds evil in everything, for his dirty mind and rebellious heart color all he sees and hears.

DECEMBER 21

Matthew 4:8-10 & Hebrews 2:18

L	D	The devil showed him all the kingdoms of the world and their splendor "all this I will give you," he said, "If you will bow down and worship me." Jesus said to him, away from me, Satan. Because he himself, suffered when he was tempted he is able to help those who are being tempted.
I	E	Matthew 4:1-11 Then the devil left him and behold, angels came and ministered to him.
V	V	2 Corinthians 5:21 Christ had no sin, but God made him become sin so that in Christ we could become right with God.
E	I	Psalm 40:8 My God, I want to do what you want your teachings are in my heart.
D	L	Luke 5:16 (NIV) Jesus often withdrew to lonely places and prayed.

DECEMBER 22

Claiming Your New Position

**Scripture Reading Colossians 3:1-17 Key Verse
Colossians 3:3**

You died, and your life is hidden with Christ in God.

Although financial poverty can occur through uncontrollable events, spiritual poverty is inexcusable for any born-again Christian.

Because we have been placed in Christ by God, we have constant, unlimited access to the Source of all spiritual blessings.

Why, then, do some walk well beneath the high calling of Scripture? Why do too many Christians suffer spiritual lack—living in personal defeat and disobedience?

The primary culprits that cause spiritual malnourishment are ignorance and unbelief. Our ignorance is of our resources in Christ. We fail to realize we are no longer habitual sinners, but justified saints.

But we must believe. Unbelief will always keep Christians mired in spiritual poverty. As long as you think of yourself in nonbiblical terms, suffering from self-condemnation and self-pity, you will not experience the joy, peace, and power that come from faith in Jesus Christ. You are a wealthy saint. God has a high calling for you.

By faith and a scriptural confession of what God's Word says about you, claim your extravagant, new position in Christ.

Lord, on the basis of Your Word and by faith, I claim my new position in Christ. I am wealthy. You have a high and noble calling for me. I rejoice in my spiritual riches.

Written by Charles Stanley

DECEMBER 23

Praise To God

Hebrews 13:15 – Let us always offer to God our sacrifice of praise.

You are a Great God
Your character is holy.
Your truth is absolute.
Your strength is unending.
Your discipline is fair.

Your provisions are abundant for our needs.
Your light is adequate for our path.
Your grace is sufficient for our sins.

You are never early, never late.
You sent your Son in the fullness of time and your plan is perfect.
Bewildering, puzzling, troubling
But perfect.

"He Reminded Us of You"
(A Prayer for A Friend)

(Winter Begins)

DECEMBER 24

Moving God's Direction

By: Charles Stanley (Book: On Holy Ground)

Have you ever felt a silent time in your walk with the Lord, a time when you did not feel in close fellowship with him? Maybe it had been weeks since your last devotional and prayer time, or perhaps you were so busy in general that your thoughts never turned to God during the bustle of the day. This is not such an unusual problem; many believers have the same experience over the course of their relationship with Christ. And the old saying is true: "God hasn't moved; you have." God is the same yesterday, today, and forever, and his love never diminishes."

DECEMBER 25

A Renewed Hearted

Create in me a clean heart, O God, and renew a steadfast Spirit within me.

Charles Stanley quoted: The feeling of distance is the result of an unquietness in your heart, which may stem from many spiritual causes. As you pray for understanding, God will show you the heart blockage. In her book when God whispers Carole Mayhill offers a prayer, based on Psalm 51.

Create in me a caring heart – tender towards the hurts happenings of others, more concerned with their needs than my own.

Create in me an attentive heart – able to hear your whisper and moment by moment to listen to your voice.

Create in me a contented heart – at peace with the circumstances of life.

Create in me a hungry heart – longing to love you more, desiring your word, reading, stretching for more of you.

(Christmas Day)

DECEMBER 26

The WORD

James 1:22-24

Do not merely listen to the Word, and so deceive yourselves. Do what is says. Anyone who listens to the Word but does not do what it says is like a man who looks at his face in a mirror and...goes away and immediately forgets what he looks like.

Psalm 119:9, 11, 72, 93

How can a young man keep his way pure? By living according to your Word. I have hidden your Word in my heart that I might not sin against you...the law from your mouth is more precious to me than thousands of pieces of silver and gold....I will never forget you precepts, for by them you have renewed my life.

DECEMBER 27

The WORD

"The scriptures are given not to increase our knowledge, but to change our lives." (Dwight Moody)

2 Timothy 3:16 (TLB)

The whole Bible was given to us by inspiration from God and is useful to teach us what is true and to make us realize what is <u>wrong in our lives</u>; it straightens us out and helps us do what is right.

DECEMBER 28

How to Listen to the Voice of God

Exodus 15:26 (TLB)

If you will listen to the voice of the Lord your God and obey it, and do what is right, then I will not make you suffer the diseases I sent on the Egyptians, for I am the Lord who heals you.

DECEMBER 29

Listen for His Voice

Let me state something important. There is never a time which Jesus is not speaking. Never! There is <u>never</u> a place in which Jesus is not present. Never! There is never a room so dark...a lounge so sensual....an office so sophisticated... that the ever-present, ever-pursuing, relentlessly tender friend is not there, tapping gently on the doors of our hearts – waiting to be invited in.

Few hear his voice. Fewer still open the door. But never interpret our numbness as his absence. For amidst the fleeting promises of pleasure is that the timeless promise of his presence. "Surely I am with you always to the very end of the age." (Matthew 28:20 NIV)

There is no chorus so loud that the voice of God cannot be heard...If we will but listen. (In the Eye of the Storm)

DECEMBER 30

Prayerful Thinking

Prayerful thinking is not unique to Augustine. David pondered the beauty of creation and felt compelled to worship his Creator: When I consider your heavens the work of your fingers, the moon and the stars, which you have ordained what is man that you are mindful of him? (Psalm 8:3-4)

As we walk life's journey, our deep thoughts and feelings and our praying can be interwoven. Seeing the beauty of nature, solving a problem can be opportunities for prayerful thinking. -- (Dennis Fisher)

Augustine was one of the most brilliant Christian thinkers of all time. Interestingly, he did some of his most effective and intimate praying while engaged in deep thought. He was what might be called a prayerful thinker. Often Augustine began a line of reasoning, and then concluded it with a prayer. Here is a sample from confessions of one of his work on theology: Too late came I to love you, O Beauty both ancient and every new; too late came I to love you...You called to me; yes, you even broke open my deafness. Your beams shined unto me and cast away my blindness. These are not the dry musing of some pseudo – theologian or armchair philosopher; they are the thoughts of someone with a passionate prayer life.

Thoughts to Ponder

What does it mean that God has "crowned man with glory and honor?"

What does that mean for me today at work and at home?

Prayerful thinking leads to purposeful thinking.

DECEMBER 31

The Light Ahead

John 8:12
I am the light of the world he that followeth me shall not walk in darkness, but shall have the light of life.

Whoso draws nigh to God one step through doubting him, God will advance a mile in blazing light to him.

The poor man is not he who is without a cent, but he who is with a dream. (Harry Kemp)

Psalm 18:28 (NRSV)
It is you who light my lamp; the Lord my God, lights up my darkness.

The evening of a well-spent life brings its lamps with it. (Joseph Jovbert)

Acknowledgements

Uplifting the Spirits of My Sisters and Brothers
Jacqueline Lofton

A Heart Like Yours
Cece Winans

Hidden Treasures of the Heart
Bishop Donald Downing

Just Like Jesus
Max Lucado

A Righteous Heart is the Fountain of Beauty
David Riper

Inner Beauty
Orsborn

The Plan of God
Horace Bughnell

When Christ Comes
Max Lucado

On Holy Ground
Charles Stanley

Upmost for His Highest
Oswald Chambers

<u>Acknowledgements</u>

Antique Rose Teapot
Henry van Dyke/Zondervan

Friend Choose Life
Bishop T. D. Jakes

Tea Time Thoughts
Edgar A. Guest/Tyndale

Climate for Healing
Dr. Robert L. Bryan, Jr.

Christ Body Was A Real Body
Dr. Robert L. Bryan, Jr.

You Must Trust
Barbour and Company, Inc.

CUMDA, 2005
The Calendar People

ComeTo Me In The Blessed Sacrament
MBS

He Is Risen
Resurrection Sunday Program April 2006
Sword of the Spirit Ministries

References

Unless otherwise indicated, all Scripture are taken from the *King James Version* of the Bible.

Scripture quotations marked *AMP* are taken from the Amplified Bible. Copyright © 1954, 1958, 1962, 1964, 1965, 1987 by the Lockman Foundation. Used by permission. (www.Lockman.org)

Verses marked *TLB* are taken from *The Living Bible*, copyright © 1971. Used by permission by Tyndale House Publishers, Inc. Wheaton, Illinois 60189. All rights reserved.

Scripture quotations marked *MSG* are taken from the Message Bible. Copyright © 2004 by the NAV Press. Used by permission.

Scripture quotations marked *NASB* are taken from the *New American Standard Bible*, Copyright © 1960, 1962, 1963, 1968, 1971, 1972, 1975, 1977 by The Lockman Foundation. Used by permission.

Scripture quotations marked *NIV* are taken from the *Holy Bible, New International Version® NIV®*. Copyright © 1973, 1978, 1984 by International Bible Society. Used by permission of Zondervan Publishing House. All rights reserved.

Scripture quotations marked *NRSV* are taken from *The New Revised Standard Version*, copyright © 1989 by the Division of Christian Education of the churches of Christ in the United States of America and is used by permission.

Printed in the United States
62556LVS00002B/25-81